The Myth of Dying

by Linda M. McCarthy, Ph.D.

THE MYTH OF DYING

Copyright © 2020 by Linda M. McCarthy, Ph.D.

Published by Lava Libros Press

Printed by IngramSpark

Edited by Mary L. Holden

Cover design and interior typography by
Diane M. Serpa at GreyCatDot Digital Design

Print ISBN: 978-1-7345749-0-6
Ebook ISBN: 978-1-7345749-1-3

All rights reserved. This book or any portion thereof may not be reproduced or used in any manner whatsoever without the express written permission of the publisher except for the use of brief quotations in a book review.

DEDICATION

This book is dedicated to my beloved son, Lt. Sean McCarthy. I will always be proud of you. When you were a child, I taught you life lessons. Now that you are in spirit, you are teaching me lessons about the afterlife. My love for and devotion to you continues to grow each day. Thank you for inspiring me to be a better person. I know that you are with me every step of the way on this journey. I lava you—always and forever.

To my friends and family—especially my daughter Shannon, and husband Kevin—thank you for your constant support. I love all of you.

CONTENTS

DEDICATION iii
FOREWORD vii
INTRODUCTION ix
CHAPTER 1: An Early Introduction to Death 1
CHAPTER 2: Studying for the Test 7
CHAPTER 3: An A+ in Anguish... 11
CHAPTER 4: Sean's Signs 21
CHAPTER 5: Running: Not Away, But Towards 31
CHAPTER 6: A Leave of Presence 37
CHAPTER 7: A Sister Speaks as She is Spoken To.......... 41
CHAPTER 8: The Message is the Medium 45
CHAPTER 9: Being My Own Medium…
 and a Metaphysician 49
CHAPTER 10: Research for Comfort 55
CHAPTER 11: Self-Science 61
CHAPTER 12: Did I Agree? 65
CHAPTER 13: The Energy of Love 69
CONCLUSION 75
ABOUT THE AUTHOR... 79
RESOURCE MATERIALS... 81

FOREWORD

Sometimes it is immediately apparent that people come into our lives for a reason. For me, Linda McCarthy is one of those people.

Linda's radiant turquoise eyes illuminate her intuitive, compassionate nature. She is a significant reason that Helping Parents Heal has been so successful in reaching parents and siblings throughout the United States and the world. Through her guidance of the Helping Parents Heal Caring Listeners program, she has helped hundreds, perhaps thousands, of parents to move forward and heal. The love and the connection that she shares with her son Sean have empowered her to reach out to others and let them know that they are going to experience joy in their lives once again, and also that our children are with us, every step of the way.

I am grateful that Linda is also a close friend, and that her son Sean and my children in spirit, Morgan, and Chelsea, have connected us. Sean's legacy of kindness lives on through his mom's work. Linda is dedicated to letting each one of the members of Helping Parents Heal know that they are not alone. She spends hours each day writing individual messages of hope and healing to parents on their children's birthdays and angel dates.

Thank you, Linda, for being a bright light and for sharing your gift with all of us through this book. I know that Sean is very proud.

~ Elizabeth Boisson
President and co-founder of Helping Parents Heal

INTRODUCTION

For as long as I can remember, I felt the reality I was born into was larger—that there was more to life than my limited physical body could detect. As a child, I didn't have the cognitive ability or the language to truly understand why I felt that way. All I knew was that there had to be something more than what my senses were perceiving. There was more than what I was being told about the nature of my life. I was a child living in the prevailing stories of my current family beliefs, but still felt that something was amiss.

The questions I had back then remained until a few years ago. Why is it that the answers I sought were so elusive, and yet so familiar?

***

Early in my life, I was raised in the Catholic religion and recall the constant reminder by clergy that I was born a sinner. This message was drilled into the congregation's psyche. It convinced me that if I were a good little girl, I would go to heaven after I died. If I misbehaved, then after my death, I would forever reside in an evil place called hell. I would dwell with a devil robed in red, with horns and a pitchfork, pleased to torment the souls rejected by God.

So, I fulfilled the tedious duty of going to church with my parents and siblings (as a child I had no choice) and searched for a false sense of security that I might be granted a pass to everlasting life. Like other churchgoers, I put my faith and hope into the hands of the priests.

The experience I had is a common one. Many people gave power to religion, believing it held all the answers, even if they didn't make logical sense. It was all about having 'faith.'

***

Years later, and after many experiences with death and grief, I awoke to the realization that I was the only one who could control my destiny and my relationship with spirit—not someone vested in attire sanctioned by the Vatican. I invite you to join me in challenging the Western cultural views of death and survival of consciousness that so many of us grew up with by presenting my own valid evidence.

***

There is not just one myth about death—there are many.

This book—my story and mission—dispels those long-standing myths.

CHAPTER 1

An Early Introduction to Death

Our spirit is not dependent on the brain or body. It is eternal, and no one has one sentence worth of hard evidence that it isn't.
~ Dr. Eben Alexander

While sitting in church as a child I would look up to the ceiling as the priest was reciting a sermon from the scriptures. What I saw were angelic beings sitting on what appeared to be clouds. My earliest recollection was that I'd been able to glimpse heaven or some version of it.

Outside the church, when peering upwards, if the sky was clear, I would ask, "Where did heaven go?"

No answer.

My next question would be, "And how far down are the gates of…" and then, in a whisper, because that word was not to be mentioned in my family, "…hell?" This was the illogical thinking of a curious child barely able to dress herself.

Yet, with early exposure to all that fear-based doctrine, I knew without a doubt that my dad would always be there to protect and keep me safe. He and I were very close; in fact, I was his shadow. I still recall the many times he'd prop me on his lap as we sat in the driver's seat of our car and he drove around the neighborhood. With my hands tightly gripping the wheel, I beamed with joy as he told me I was the best driver ever. Even with a steering wheel that was as big as I was, the thrill of turning it made me squeal with delight. "When can I drive again daddy?" I'd whisper in his ear when we got home. The warmth of his laughter, and the tenderness of his hugs, lingered long after my early driving lessons were over.

***

One day in the midst of my early years, I was standing on a stool looking out a window at my dad as he was washing the car. I saw him clutch his chest and fall to the ground. I pounded on the window and remember saying, "Daddy get up!" and then I yelled, "Daddy fell down!" What I was seeing was sudden and unexpected. It was not my dad's usual routine of waving to me as he pointed the hose at the window.

When my mom ran outside, I vividly recall the guttural scream emanating from her body. It was unlike anything that I had ever heard, and it frightened me. It was primordial, and one that I hope to never hear again.

My dad was lying dead on the ground from an apparent heart attack.

Mom called dad's sister, my aunt Louise. She, uncle Jack, and cousin Joyce, lived close by. I was kept at bay, unable to reach him. An ambulance arrived as he lay there on the ground. The medics put a sheet over his lifeless body and lifted him into the vehicle. At that time, cardiopulmonary resuscitation was just being discovered and not in general use. I never had the chance to say goodbye or give him one last kiss.

Aunt Louise, uncle Jack, and Joyce tried to console my mother. She was hysterical and in shock. My aunt lost her brother, my mom lost her husband, and my siblings and I lost our dad. Now what? We were sinking into the abyss of shock, loss, grief, profound sorrow…and the unknown.

My family was large and blended. When my parents met, they were raising children from prior unions; after their marriage, my three brothers, sister, and I were born. A number of the other children were living outside our home by the time I arrived.

Everyone gathered for my dad's funeral. I have very little recall about that day. In fact, no one ever discussed it. What I do remember was one of my brothers telling me that my dad was sleeping, and not to wake him. Another older half-brother held me in his arms as we slowly walked up to view dad in his casket. Ignoring his request, I kept saying, "Wake up, daddy, wake up." I noticed people sobbing and wondered why they were crying and why was he sleeping in a box in church. He looked so peaceful and handsome in his suit.

My dad had been employed as a long-haul truck driver for a company called Pacific Intermountain Express (P-I-E) in California. I was the one designated to go and wake him up for dinner after he got back from one of his long trips. This scenario seemed very odd, yet familiar. I was supposed to be the one to wake him up! Unable to arouse him from deep slumber, I was whisked away, told to go play, and was treated like nothing had happened.

However, something had happened. My dad had died. Why wasn't anyone recognizing it?

***

In the weeks following my dad's death, I was afraid to fall asleep for fear that I too would be put into a box. My brothers taunted me by telling me if I didn't go to bed, a huge white flying horse would sweep down and carry me away. That horse was a logo for a gas company. I would lie in bed, eyes shut tight, hoping the horse couldn't sense that I was still awake. Eventually my body would succumb to exhaustion, and I would fall asleep.

***

A few months after my dad passed, we moved from Los Angeles, California to Phoenix, Arizona. Our family already owned a home there. It was a place where my mom went to live when her asthma flared. The dry desert climate alleviated her symptoms. She felt the move was a better option for all of us, and the weather was more conducive to her good health. My beloved grandma lived nearby. She helped manage us kids and gave emotional support to my mom.

It was a challenging transition for my family, but grandma Rose was always there to catch us when we stumbled. She truly was amazing, and a lifeline when we were all feeling lost and confused. With her guidance and support, our scattered lives returned to some normalcy in Phoenix.

On Sundays, we would walk as a family to the local Catholic church, only a few blocks away. I remember dreading what sin I might have committed that week, even though I was only 5 years old. I was anxious that the priest would somehow get the lowdown on any bad behavior I may have done. After all, the priest had a direct line to God, and he was the one to administer punishment. My anxiety level would soar, and I would find myself holding my breath in anticipation. Sometimes I wished I would pass out so I wouldn't have to experience the possible ramifications of my actions, whatever they happened to be that week. I never received more than a finger-wagging, but to a child, it was more than enough.

In Mass, it seemed to always be the same lecture about being a good person, following God's laws, and behaving for parents. I would rather have heard a homily about being a good person in accordance to God's word, but instead I prayed to become invisible so the priest couldn't see me. I was self-inflicting my own punishments of guilt and shame. It was a feeling of despair even at that young age. Perhaps I felt guilty for somehow not being able to save my dad as he lay dying on the ground.

One particular service stands out in my young mind; it was when the priest offered prayers for members of the congregation who'd died. I remember thinking that since my dad had been a good person, he'd be in heaven with God and the angels. That thought was the motivation I needed to be a good little girl so I could see my dad again after I left this world. Questions were swirling in my head. How good did I need to be? Who would decide my fate? God? The priest? My family?

As weeks turned into months, the stress of grief was too much for my mom to manage. Alcohol became her respite and caring for all the children was more than she could tolerate. The house no longer felt like a home to me, and with inconsistent meals, we hid what food we could find. The house was in turmoil. My younger sister was just a baby at the time, and I'm sure she took a lot of mom's attention. My brothers and I were sent outside to play all day. We had the good fortune to have a park across the street and went there for entertainment and shelter from the sun. We also went to grandma's house where we would get hugs, and slices of her delicious pies. We could smell them even before we reached her door as they cooled on the window ledge. Then we'd go back home in the late afternoons or early evenings, exhausted and ready for sleep.

Every day was a repeat of the last, until one day I left to go back to Los Angeles to spend time with aunt Louise, uncle Jack, and Joyce. I liked visiting them and did not want to return to Arizona. It was peaceful there; more like a home.

When I did return to my mom's house, I was unhappy. I remember thinking "This isn't a home without my daddy." After long conversations with my mom, aunt Louise asked if I would like to come live with them for a little while. We were always very close, and it was so much fun to get the attention I craved. So, when aunt Louise asked if she could take me until things settled down, mom was more than happy to oblige. For her, it meant one less mouth to feed, one less body to clothe. Going back to live with them in California was a gift from my dad. I knew it. I was back in the neighborhood and with a family that I loved.

***

Since I'd spent so much time visiting their house when my dad was alive, living with aunt Louise, uncle Jack, and Joyce appeared to be a seamless transition. What no one realized at the time was that I was a highly sensitive child. Adapting wasn't easy. Acclimating to a new home environment, school, and friends was challenging. At times, I would awake with blood under my fingernails, my skin ripped open from scratching. My anxiety was often so high that I'd crawl onto the edge of the bed with my aunt Louise and hold her toe to fall asleep. Honestly, I don't know how she tolerated it. Although I experienced the trauma of my dad's passing, I don't think the enormity of the loss was part of my reality yet.

I remember many nights in the quiet of my room, wondering where my dad was because no one ever spoke about his passing. Death was a subject that was sidestepped. All I knew was that he went to heaven and was with God. Many times, I asked where this place called heaven was. How high was it? How did a person get there? Why did God take my daddy? I could never find answers, no matter how many times I asked. I loved him so much. It wasn't fair. I wanted him back! Sometimes, in the darkness of my room I thought I could sense him nearby. It would frighten me, and I'd put the covers over my head. Then the sensations stopped. The last thing a parent wants to do—even one who is in spirit—is scare their child.

Aunt Louise, uncle Jack, and Joyce did not attend church on a regular basis, so the questions that I pondered in the darkness of my room eventually dissipated into oblivion. I had other important things to do, like play with friends, and go to school. I loved school. Life became normal, as I acclimated to my environment, and soon I began to think of Louise and Jack as parents, and Joyce as a big sister. I had a family who loved me, and I felt safe. Los Angeles was once again my permanent home.

CHAPTER 2
Studying for the Test

There is an afterlife. I am convinced of this.
~ Paulo Coelho

The years in elementary school went by and I didn't think too much about death until I was in sixth grade. My teacher, Mr. Burke, gave us a research assignment. I chose to study, and even draw a re-creation of, the Aztec Sun (Calendar) Stone because I was fascinated with Native American culture and beliefs. It was part of my ancestry and I wanted to know everything about it. This relic was discovered in Mexico City in 1790, but it was carved in 1479 from a piece of basalt. It is three feet thick, nearly 12 feet wide, and weighs over 22 tons.

The Aztecs worshipped many Gods, not just one, and saw God in everything. What an amazing perspective this was to me. They also had a strong belief in the afterlife and reincarnation. That resonated with me on a deep spiritual level, even though I couldn't define it in my limited vocabulary.

This ancient Aztec prayer touched my heart, even at that young age:

Only for so short a while you have loaned us to each other,
because we take form in your act of drawing us,
and we take life in your painting us, and we breathe in your singing us.
But only for so short a while have you loaned us to each other.
Because even a drawing cut in obsidian fades,
and the green feathers, the crown feathers, of the Quetzal bird lose their color,
and even the sounds of the waterfall die out in the dry season.
So, we too, because only for a short while have you loaned us to each other.

After the project was completed, I covertly read books on what happens after death although the library's selection was quite limited, and most were religious in context. The continual regurgitation of, "You are born a sinner, and you will be judged before you are able to enter the kingdom of heaven. If you are rejected, you will go to hell," echoed in my mind.

One question continued to challenge me: "How good did I have to be?" Not one of the books I'd read had the answer to that mysterious question. In fact, with the inadequate amount of information available to me, it created more questions than answers. So much confusion swirled around in my young brain.

I recalled stories I'd been told about the process of death and dying. Many seemed illogical. For example, I was told that people who'd died lay dormant in their graves, awaiting the eventual return of Jesus to resurrect them. The chosen ones would break free from their entombment and ascend to their heavenly home. Or, after crossing over, souls wait patiently at the entrance to the Pearly Gates for Saint Peter to grant either a thumbs-up (heaven) or a thumbs-down (hell).

How could one single saint determine my eternal life? And where was God in all of this? Is this the game of life—of everlasting life? Where is hell located? Is it in the center of planet Earth with swirling molten lava? Is it possible to spend eternity there with no way of getting out? And what about purgatory? Is purgatory some type of limbo where the dead reside until enough prayers are said to pay their ransom to proceed to heaven? How many prayers does one require? Who is, and will be, praying for me?

The religion I was taught demanded belief in a dogma that made no room for examination. There seemed to be no escape either way and my questions were never-ending. If God loves people so much, why in the world would He send them someplace horrific for eternity? The biblical interpretation was either black or white, with no shades of grey.

***

Eventually I stopped asking questions since it made people uneasy and defensive. No one seemed to have any answers that made logical sense to me anyway. I surrendered my search, assuming adults knew something that I wasn't privy to. After all, they were supposedly far more knowledgeable about these things. I made a decision to focus on school, and on my friends, and to forget about anything spiritual. I felt as if I were once again being pulled back into the confinement of the limited beliefs of others, and yet I surrendered willingly.

My life path became one of completing my education, establishing a career, getting married, and eventually starting a family. I didn't have any more time or energy to waste pondering the secrets of the universe. Evidently, they were secrets for a reason.

However, in 1999, a spark was reignited and renewed my interest in the survival of consciousness after death. I had no idea why the subject was now at the forefront of my quest to understand its meaning once again. It was like being awakened from a deep slumber with an insatiable hunger for answers to questions I had pondered my whole life. Little did I realize that this hunger, and the resulting quest, would one day save my sanity, and perhaps even my life.

As an adult, I looked for mentors to help me explore my renewed passion for belief in the continuation of consciousness after death. I wanted to understand the human body's energy systems. I was fortunate to find a job with a company that helped me unravel some of the mysteries that eluded me all those years.

It was with a wonderful group of practitioners at a wellness center called Natural Healing in Annapolis, Maryland that I found support for my mission. On staff was an acupuncturist who taught me about the energy meridians in the body, and how important they are to overall health. I also met Kendra, who was at that time a talented, up-and-coming yoga instructor and reiki practitioner; she now is known as a "spirit medic." She is still a wonderful friend of mine who graciously shares her wisdom with me about the spiritual realm as well as her knowledge of energy fields in the body.

At the same time, I studied with the British Institute of Homeopathy, an entity focused on energy medicine. I met a few naturopaths who implemented Applied Kinesiology (AK), which I found fascinating. AK, also known as muscle strength testing, is a method of diagnosis and treatment based on the belief that various muscles are linked to particular organs and glands, and that specific muscle weakness can signal distant internal problems such as nerve damage, reduced blood supply, chemical imbalances, or other organ or gland problems.

For wellness, we employed yoga instructors, massage therapists, and for spiritual growth, a shaman was on staff. What is a shaman? I discovered that a shaman acts as an intermediary between the physical and non-physical worlds. The shaman's name was Ronnie, and she and I had many lively conversations. She imparted her years of knowledge and shared her visions of the unseen world—that of the spiritual realm. Through all these amazing individuals as well as others, I learned an incredible amount about my physical body, mind, and most importantly, my spiritual body.

My love of afterlife anecdotes and survival of consciousness after death theories was voracious. I devoured book after book and hungered for more. I was never satiated. I know my family must have thought I was crazy. Why in the world was I interested in the non-physical world and energy? I had no logical answer, even for myself.

CHAPTER 3

An A+ in Anguish

*I am convinced of the afterlife, independent of theology.
If the world is rationally constructed, there must be an afterlife.*
~ Kurt Gödel

All of this wisdom and knowledge was put to the most difficult test in June of 2014 when my beloved son, Sean, transitioned back to spirit at the age of 27.

***

As a naval officer, Sean had just achieved the rank of lieutenant and was embarking on a new assignment with Navy Special Warfare in Virginia Beach. He was in the process of furnishing a home of his own and lived two blocks from

My wonderful son, Sean Patrick McCarthy, 1987-2014.

the beach. When it was quiet, he could hear the sound of waves breaking along the shoreline. His previous apartment in San Diego was also in close proximity to the beach. Living by the water was important to him; it soothed his empathic spirit.

His new place had a washer and dryer in a small laundry room, and he was overjoyed. We laughed about how the first thing he did after arriving was a load of dirty clothes from his long drive across the country. No longer did he have to go outside to retrieve his laundry like he had to do in California.

***

Sean loved making people laugh. With his heart of gold, he'd give anyone the shirt off his back. He was a loving spirit from birth, and throughout his life, he showed the many ways he cared for others and their needs.

When Sean was about 6 or 7 years old, his aunt Kathy took both him and his sister Shannon to New York City and they visited the FAO Schwarz toy store. I had given each of them money, small bills, so they could purchase a toy. By the time they'd walked to the store, Sean was almost completely out of the money. Kathy asked him what had happened, and he said that he had given it to homeless people because they needed it more than he did. Even as a child, he would always lend a helping hand.

***

The week before he was supposed to check in to his new duty station in Virginia Beach, Sean drove from San Diego to Phoenix to spend a week with our family. I was so happy to see him, since he had previously been on an eight-month deployment, and the Navy kept him quite busy even when he was back on shore duty. That week with him was a precious gift, and I will always cherish it.

At the end of that week, after shopping for items for his new apartment, playing golf with his dad, Kevin, and just enjoying some down time, Sean drove for three-and-a-half days back to Virginia Beach. He was excited to move into his new place and start his assignment in naval special warfare. This assignment meant a lot to him. He had so much to do in a short time but was fortunate to have friends who were also assigned there; a couple of them even stopped by to welcome him to the area.

I remember our last conversation like it was yesterday. He called me as I was shopping for plants at Home Depot. He asked if he should buy a king or queen size bed. His room was big enough to accommodate a king, but I told him to consider the queen so he would have more space. He agreed and bought it that afternoon. Along with his other purchases was a new flat screen TV to watch the World Cup soccer game with his friends that weekend. Grocery shopping was next on his list, and then buying a beach bike for sunset rides. We agreed that we would call one another every couple of days just to touch base. His belongings were due to arrive from the Navy that week and he was excited to have a place with his own new furnishings.

When I hadn't heard from him, I assumed it was because he had movers coming and a lot to do before starting work on Monday. Moving is always hectic and he had a propensity to misplace his phone. I began to worry when I hadn't heard from him on day four. He always called me on Sundays, but I put my worries aside, thinking that with the World Cup going on, and having friends over, the evening might have run quite late. I was also opening a new office and was busy with all the details of decorating and paperwork. Still, something didn't feel right. I brushed it aside, thinking it was just me being a mom who worried too much, but my instincts knew otherwise. My stomach churned and my thoughts raced later that night when I still hadn't heard from him. Not even a text. Something wasn't right.

The following Monday around 10 o'clock in the morning, I received a call from a woman Sean had been seeing. She hadn't heard from him and wondered if I had spoken with him. Since she was also in the military, she had the ability to call the base where he was about to begin the first day of his new assignment. When she called, she was told that Sean was there, doing a walk around to become familiar with the facility and they would ask him to call her, or us, when he returned.

Hours went by and there was no call. Kevin and I asked the police do a wellness visit and they told us that his car was still in the apartment parking lot. Why would his car still be in the parking lot when we were told he was at the base? My stomach dropped and I felt sick. Someone wasn't telling us the truth.

Minutes seemed like hours that morning before we received a call from the police detective who asked me in a very matter of fact tone: "Is your son Sean McCarthy?"

"Yes," I responded, my voice quivering.

"I'm sorry to inform you that we found him deceased in his apartment. We are in the process of conducting an investigation, and the military will be contacting you for further instructions."

I could feel the life force draining out of me. Anguished, I cried out, "NO. NO. NO. That's not possible."

It's difficult to articulate the depth of despair that I felt at that moment, as my muscles stiffened in an attempt to keep my body from collapsing onto the kitchen floor. Life as I knew it, would never be the same. A part of me died that day.

Things became a blur at that point. I was in shock, but remember saying, "Let's go bring Sean home." I didn't want him in an unfamiliar place with strangers. He needed to be home with his family.

We awaited details from the Navy on how to proceed.

Just like in the movies, there was a knock at our door. I knew I would see a chaplain standing there, stoic, prepared to tell us our beloved son had died. When I opened the door, I said, "I already know."

The Navy representatives came into our home and took us through the process of transportation and arrangements for Sean.

Arrangements? I was supposed to go help arrange his apartment with new furniture—not plan his funeral! It all sounded so organized and official. I know they were just doing their job, but it felt cold and void of any emotion—until a lieutenant, who was named Micah, gave me a gentle hug on his way out the door.

After the officials left, the guard at the entrance to our community called and expressed his sympathies. Sean had worked as a guard there during the summers of his college years. We held our breath as we called our daughter Shannon in California to give her the information we were trying to absorb. The Navy officials had offered to send a representative to her, but I asked them not to add to the trauma she'd feel after we called her. She was devastated and made immediate plans to fly to Phoenix to be with us.

I don't recall the drive to the airport to pick up Shannon; my head was in a fog. I couldn't gather the strength to meet her as she exited the plane. I sat alone in an empty area so that I could cry without people staring at me. Quiet tears of devastation stained my cheeks. All of our hearts were shattered. There was a huge hole in my heart. I felt like I was hemorrhaging, and I wasn't sure I would survive…or wanted to survive.

Sean was our youngest, and only son.

We three—Kevin, Shannon, and I—headed for the airport chapel. I remember that it was a long trek, almost to the other end of the terminal. I said to God, "If this is a nightmare, please wake me up. If this is real, please God, give me the strength to endure." At that point, I barely had the energy to walk. My legs felt like I was dragging weights behind them, all I wanted to do was curl up into a ball and never wake up.

How could I go through the rest of my life without my precious son? Sean and I had a bond that was special, different than any relationship I have ever had. We could read each other's thoughts. Sean's highly intuitive ability let him perceive life in a way that many of his contemporaries didn't understand. In fact, it wasn't unusual for them to turn to him for advice. He willingly gave it—heart and soul. He would stay up all night consoling a despondent friend, making sure they were OK before leaving for work the next morning. That's the type of man he was.

***

The next day, a Tuesday, we flew to Virginia Beach. The same incomprehensible question kept echoing in my mind: "Why would he have been sleeping in his apartment when he had booked a room at the Holiday Inn until Friday?" He had no furniture, or essentials like towels to even take a shower, just clothes from his luggage.

I kept recalling a conversation we had as he was traveling to Virginia Beach when he'd said, "Mom, I am getting a hotel room until my furniture arrives. I am not sleeping on the floor." The rest of his belongings were all packed by the Navy. In fact, I had sent him a beach towel and it was still in his mailbox when we arrived there on Tuesday. It was clear he wasn't yet residing at the apartment.

I was still attempting to wrap my head around the fact that I wasn't going to see him alive again. My head felt like it was going to explode with questions that I could find no logical answers to.

The flight across the country seemed to take forever. As soon as we arrived at the hotel that evening, the paperwork began. There were copious stacks of forms to fill out, and we had very little time to plan a service. It was less than a week before the fourth of July holiday. With the help of family and friends, word got out to those who could attend Sean's funeral on short notice.

I kept thinking that I would awaken from that terrible nightmare. "Please God, make it go away!" I prayed time and time again, to no avail.

As the late evening hours passed, I knew it would begin all over again early the next morning. It had been an exhausting day, but my brain couldn't shut down.

It was in a primal emotional state; one that only a parent who has had this experience can truly understand. I feared for the mother in me. The loss was so vast that my mind recoiled at the truth. The pain was searing inside my body, like a hot coal. Would I be able to manage this, or would I succumb to the enormity of the situation and die of a broken heart? At that point, I truly didn't care. I just wanted the pain to cease. I felt like I was living in a state of suspended animation. The immense weight of grief surrounded my body and mind, with no exit point.

I once read that the loss of a child is so great there is no name for it. In a marriage when a spouse dies, the wife becomes a widow, the husband, a widower. A child whose parents die is an orphan. There is no name for a parent who has lost a child. Now I understood why.

When the paperwork was complete, I remember collapsing on the floor of the hotel room. There would be at least three long days ahead, and I had to get myself together for the sake of my family. I just kept repeating: "If anyone is out there, please help me!"

Then something unusual happened.

When I opened my luggage, a large white feather, 12 inches long, was laying neatly across my clothes. How did a feather, especially one that big, get into my luggage? I picked it up, stunned, as I had no idea how it got there. I knew I had to keep that feather with me, as a pacifier, to soothe my soul. The feather was the only tangible item I could hold onto at the time. Little did I realize that it was the beginning of a beautiful new relationship with those in the spirit realm.

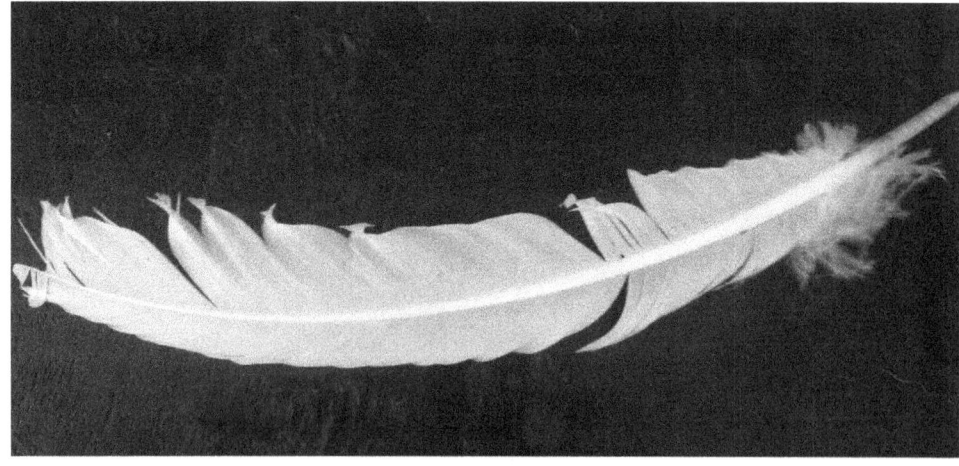

Feather found inside my luggage.

The next day, the assigned officers drove us from location to location, before ending up at the garage where Sean parked his car for the last time. There were still a number of the items he had yet to unpack, like golf clubs, since he had only been there for a few days. The chief asked if I wanted anything from his car.

"His Buddha and his crystal!" I blurted out with the authority of a drill instructor. Everyone looked at me like I'd said something bizarre. How would I know that he had a Buddha and a crystal in his car? I walked over, and there on the console was a tiny Buddha statue and a beautiful clear quartz crystal. I gripped them for dear life, knowing that only a few days earlier, he had held them in his hands. They had kept him company on the cross-country drive. In fact, he never went anywhere without them.

Sean resonated more with the Buddhism than Catholicism. It was a philosophy, not a religion to him. We both loved this anonymous saying: "Buddha was not a Buddhist. Jesus was not a Christian. Muhammad was not a Muslim. They were teachers who taught Love…Love was their religion." Both he and I read books on Buddhism and enjoyed the teachings. They were all about love, and how to live a moral life, to be mindful and aware of one's thoughts and actions, and to develop wisdom and in order to understand life.

I knew I wanted to keep this tiny Buddha and crystal close to me. In the process of packing up all his belongings, being so small, these items surely would have gotten lost. They were important to Sean, and even more important to me now. He'd carried them along with an animal totem I had given him for safety when he was on deployment. Now, to me, they were precious mementos of his life.

***

We visited the funeral home to decide what verses would be read at his service. Sean wanted to be cremated, and I am forever grateful that we had that conversation before he left for deployment. We choose the pictures to be displayed in the chapel, made sure they had his dress whites, and all other details confirmed. They asked if we would like to have a ring made with his fingerprint. We all thought that was a wonderful way to keep Sean close to us. I am very thankful for the guidance we received at the funeral home. Now when I touch my ring, I feel like I am touching Sean's finger, and in a way, I am.

***

After a full day of planning, we headed back to the hotel. Family and friends were waiting there. Spirit was about to make itself known again. Joyce grabbed a can of Coke from the snack bar. At that time, there were first names printed on the cans. She paid for it, turned it around, and saw the name Sean. It was like a gentle hello from spirit. In hindsight, I wish I had saved it. What are the chances that the name Sean would be printed on a can of soda at a hotel lobby snack bar?

I was grateful that my best friend (and soul sister) Ann was there to meet me in Virginia Beach. She did everything she could to help me, even bringing me melatonin because sleep eluded me. I kept waking up in that hotel room with the realization of why I was there. Tears flowed as I sobbed into the pillow, praying that this was a terrible nightmare, yet knowing it was not.

***

On the second morning, right before dawn, I finally dozed off into a deep slumber and had my first dream visitation from Sean. It was definitely a visitation, not a regular dream, because I remember it to this day. In the dream, Sean was standing at what appeared to be a train station. He was behind a metal turnstile, but I could see his face. He was in his Navy dress whites, and his smile was beaming. Sean looked so handsome, as he stood there. He was holding a baby in his arms, and he said, "I have to go home now, mom."

There was sadness in my dream voice as I said, "I know, I know," and then watched as Sean and the baby faded away into the light mist that surrounded them. (Later, a well-known evidential medium told me that the baby Sean was carrying was the child that I had miscarried years before. He had his brother with him and wanted me to know that they were together. My two boys were reunited in spirit.)

***

Sean's funeral took place that morning. There were more people than I expected with such a short amount of time to get the word out, and I was grateful for their presence. Military personnel videotaped the service, from opposite sides of the chapel. I never saw the footage, even though I was offered a copy. Perhaps it was misplaced due to the hurried schedule that surrounded the timing of his service.

I thanked the commanding officer of the Navy Special Warfare base for the expeditious work in which his team had created a beautiful ceremony honoring Sean, especially since he never had the opportunity to work with our son.

His response: "Unfortunately we are experts at this because we do them more often than we would like," took me aback. It was disheartening to hear, to say the least.

I was told by one of Sean's former superior officers after the service that he'd felt proud to pin another Navy Achievement Medal on Sean. We knew he had been awarded one, but we were not aware he had two of them. Integrity, and living a life of service, were two of Sean's best qualities.

After everyone left, I stepped outside to get some air. I felt as if all the oxygen had been siphoned out of the room and I was gasping to take a breath. I failed to pay proper attention to all the butterflies, dragonflies, and hummingbirds that surrounded me. Looking back, I now recognize that they were gentle signs from the spiritual realm to let me know that we were not alone, and all was well.

***

Now, my mission was to bring Sean back home to Arizona. As we prepared to leave for the airport to return home, I held on for dear life to the urn that contained his ashes. No one was going to take it from me. I found myself putting it on my hip and rocking him back and forth, just like I did when he was a baby. Sean would always be my baby boy. As his mom, I was protecting him, even if he was encased in an urn.

The rules are stringent for bringing back the cremains of a loved one, so I was grateful that we had a military escort. A chief from Navy Special Warfare and a chaplain accompanied us back to Arizona. I thought that perhaps the chaplain might come but did not expect to have two escorts. I wasn't sure if this was standard protocol, but I was grateful for their companionship. They stayed in Arizona for a couple of days after we arrived home to complete unfinished business.

Even with their paperwork, and them being in uniform, the going-home process was challenging. The airlines were very respectful, giving us priority to land during the first leg so that we could catch a connecting flight. I didn't want to put Sean's ashes in the overhead bin, but it was a regulation. At least I had them close. I know it may sound silly, but the idea that his urn was in the overhead compartment upset me. I didn't want to let him go or be alone.

All I wanted to do was get Sean home where I knew he would be safe.

The pilot announced that a fallen soldier and his family were on board, and to please be respectful by allowing us to exit first. I heard a few quiet sobs from passengers as we awaited the opening of the aircraft door. It was all I could do to keep from bursting into tears. I bit deeply into the side of my mouth to distract myself from the pain I felt in my heart. I kept my head down, knowing that all eyes were on us.

In the terminal, as we headed for the flight back to Phoenix, I held tight to Sean's urn, pressing it close to my chest, knowing I would have to relinquish it again on the following flight.

I could hear people applauding and crying. Evidently it was announced on the speaker before we departed the aircraft that a fallen soldier was on his final flight home. I couldn't look directly at anyone because I knew I would fall apart. To stay strong in that moment, I just nodded my appreciation to the onlookers as I rushed to catch the next flight.

CHAPTER 4

Sean's Signs

I firmly believe that when you die you will enter immediately into another life. They who have gone before us are alive in one form of life and we in another.
~ Norman Vincent Peale

After we returned home, all the work of notifying companies and entities about Sean's death began. I was thankful that I had paperwork to keep me busy even if it was a task I never imagined I would have to do. Each time I explained that I was calling because my son was deceased, the person on the other end of the line would begin to cry. Tears continually flowed down my face, as I navigated the process of closing his accounts.

Days turned into weeks as I waited for Sean's belongings. I knew I wouldn't feel complete until his car was in the garage and his boxes were with us. I wondered if the delay was caused by the last conversation I had with the chief. It was very businesslike and not at all like our previous discussions. Something had changed—but what? And more important—why?

Sleeping at night was a challenge for me. Every time I closed my eyes, I could feel the panic begin swirling up in my body. All I wanted was to be close to Sean's urn in the family room, so the couch became my bed of choice. As odd as it might sound, I didn't want him to be alone, but that is the thinking of a mother engulfed in deep grief.

I hated waking up in the morning and knowing that I would have to face another day without Sean. Slowly, the reality mingled with mourning enveloped my body. I felt alone and scared. How could I face this world without my son? I needed something, anything to let me know he was OK, but logic made me realize it was only wishful thinking.

***

One evening, a week or two after his service, I said to Sean, "If you are here, please give me a sign." I truly didn't expect anything, but just talking to him aloud made me feel like he was around. I had read that it takes time for a soul to acclimate into their new reality, so perhaps all the things that happened before now were just coincidences. I didn't care, I just needed something tangible to grasp onto.

In the early hours of the morning, after pleading for a sign, a lamp next to the loveseat (that had been Sean's personal choice of place for TV watching) slowly began to glow and light up. I couldn't believe my eyes. The only way to turn on that lamp was with a switch located behind the loveseat. And the only person in the room was me. So how did the light turn on by itself? I just remember feeling so comforted that I curled up on the couch and immediately fell asleep until dawn. That was a rarity for me since I only slept in snippets and minutes, not hours.

The next morning, Kevin came into the room and turned off the light. When I awoke, he asked me why I had turned it on. He knew that I only sleep in total darkness. In fact, I normally wear a sleep mask; my eyes are sensitive, and light bothers them. I told him that I hadn't touched the light, but that it came on all by itself. As he shook his head, he probably thought I was losing my mind. All I knew was that it came on and I didn't touch it, so who, or what, did?

The following evening, I waited patiently, but the light never came back on. I concluded that the signs from Sean were over, and my heart sank with despair.

Little did I know, his spirit was just warming up.

Another night, as I lay on the couch, about to doze off, I felt the covers being pulled up over my legs. I quietly said, "Thank you," before closing my eyes for a short nap. When I awoke, I realized that there was no one else in the house. Who had pulled the covers over me? Was I hallucinating, or as I thought, making it up?

***

My encounters with spirit were accelerating. Early one morning before dawn, I went into the back yard and dangled my feet in the spa. The water was still warm since the summer evening temperatures in the Phoenix rarely go below 90 degrees. It felt like bathwater—very soothing. The sky was just beginning to change from black to a pale shade of pink. Streaks from contrails painted the horizon as the sun began to rise, and the stars faded gently into the morning light.

I began talking aloud to Sean explaining I needed a sign from him, not anyone else, in spirit. I wanted something tangible to know he heard me, and I was feeling desperate once again. As quickly as my request was sent, I heard a voice say, "Look behind the picture in the library cabinet." It was more of a whisper than a booming voice.

"Who said that?" I questioned loudly and with authority, as if someone was going to answer. "What picture in the library cabinet?" I thought as I looked around to see who was talking to me. Dear God, now I was hearing voices! Maybe I was beginning to lose my mind.

I dried my feet and went inside, not expecting to find anything that would resonate with my request. There was a picture of Sean and a friend of his from middle school that I had recently found and put in the cabinet. That wasn't what I was looking for; I knew that one was there. However, when I picked up the picture to give him a kiss, stashed behind it were three notes handwritten by Sean when he was in elementary school. One was a poem, and two were notes saying he loved me.

Sean was always writing either a poem or a note and leaving it for me. I used to leave notes for both he and Shannon. It was our way of saying "I love you," when they were at school.

I was elated and shocked. Why in the world would I have put those notes behind a picture? I'd kept these notes and pictures in boxes or plastic bags to preserve them. I lovingly read each one, with tears slowly streaming down my face,

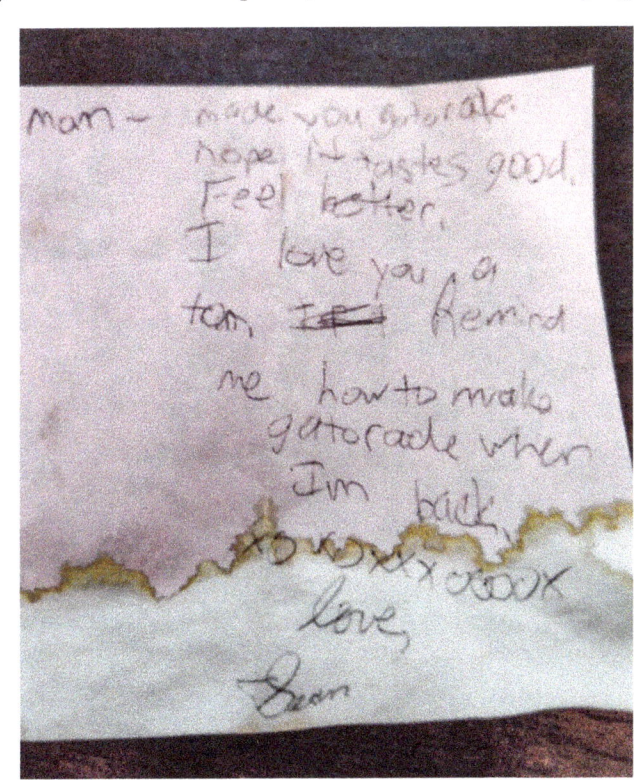

Handwritten note I found behind a picture.

and marveled at the innocence and sweetness of his words. Then I placed them next to his picture and urn. One of the tiny handwritten notes said, "I love you Mom. I hope you feel better."

***

Because I'd shared my discovery of the white feather in the suitcase with a few family and friends, they began calling to tell me of their own experiences with Sean's spirit. Joyce, who now lived in Florida, told me that she opened her front door and found a big white feather. Even though there are seagulls in Florida, this was the first time such a large white feather appeared at her front door. Friends told me they found white feathers on their car's windshield, or at their door.

I was grateful for their messages, but also wondered if they were just trying to comfort me—until I heard from my niece, Kimberly. This letter from Kimberly changed my mind. She is the type of person who needs proof, not just hearsay. Here's her letter to me:

Dear Aunt Linda,

There are no words that I can even begin to think of to tell you how truly sorry I am to hear about Sean. Such a tragedy; such a wonderful young man.

I know that my mom shared with you some of the experiences that I have had over the past week, but I wanted to relay them to you as well. Typically, every day after work, I go to the beach across from where I live. This past Monday, I started onto the beach and being distracted for some reason, I missed the turn and ended up heading north on A1A, not what I intended to do. I decided to just go to the next public access beach and pull in. As I walked onto the boardwalk, I noticed that carved into the wood it said, "Sean loves Shannon 4 ever." I rubbed my hands over the carving and smiled but kept walking.

My friend looked back and said, "Oh that's neat. It says your cousin's name."

I smiled and said, "Did I tell you that my other cousin's name is Shannon and she is Sean's sister?"

She gave me this shocked look and said, "Don't you find this really odd that you missed the turn and now you see this?"

I smiled and said, "It is a cool reminder."

She just gave me this odd look and said, "I know you say you don't believe in this kind of stuff, but you might need to open your mind to the possibility."

On Thursday, I was talking to my mom on the phone and she told me the story about you finding a white feather in your suitcase. I stepped outside my office to finish a discussion. I looked over right outside my door and there was a white feather on the ground. I said to my mom, "OMG, you are not going to believe this, but I swear I just found a white feather on the ground." I told my mom I was going to send her a picture because this was just too weird. When I came walking into my office holding the feather, everyone was asking me what I was doing. I began telling them the story, and they all had goosebumps and told me I better get with the program because someone was trying to tell me something. I was literally shaking and just left work. As I drove home, I felt this sense of peace as though all was okay.

When I got home, I sent a text to Jimmy [her brother] and asked him if he believes in psychic events. He responded, "Yes," and asked why. By then I was freaking out and didn't text him back and decided to go to the beach and unwind. When I checked my phone a bit later, he had sent me a text asking what was going on. With that, I relayed the above story to him, but he did not respond for a few hours.

When contacted me later he said, "You are not going to believe me when I tell you this, so I am going to send you a picture." He said when he couldn't get in touch with me, he assumed I was busy, so he went outside with his wife and son to sit by the fire. His son announced that he saw a blue star. Not seeing anything, Jimmy said his son Blake climbed up on the back stairs to get a better look.

Jimmy said as Blake was stepping down, he said, "Look dad, I found a white feather for you."

Jimmy said, "Oh, that is great," but didn't think much about it until he walked into the house and read my text message. He too was freaking out. He kept saying, "Obviously we are getting a message but why and what does it mean?" Jimmy said he too felt this sense that all was going to be okay. It was much like the feeling I got out of nowhere. I felt this sense of calmness.

I decided when in doubt, Google it! I was shocked to see how many references there were about white feathers being a sign from an angel that all *is well. Obviously, I am completely out of touch because this was the first time I had ever heard of this.*

Sean has convinced me that I need to expand my belief system and realize that yes, our loved ones can still stay in contact with us from beyond.

I wish there was something I could say or do to take your pain away.

Godspeed Sean Patrick!

Love,

Kimberly

Were these coincidences flukes? Perhaps, but I believe they were signs from Sean, the angels, or spirit guides to let me and my family know that they are always with us. They were working non-stop to let us all know that death is only an illusion.

While considering these signs, I remembered a long-ago conversation I had with a co-worker. Her father had just transitioned, and she believed spirit would use whatever means necessary to get a message across the veil to loved ones in grief. Spirit reveals signs to family members, friends, perhaps even to people who are new friends, and sometimes, strangers with whom a moment is shared. She'd said, "They will use any means necessary to get the message across to you."

Many years ago, when baby Sean was being fussy, I would sing a few lines from the song "Angel Baby" in his ear. It was a popular in 1961, sung by Rosie and the Originals. If you want to hear it on YouTube, here's the link: **www.youtube.com/watch?v=bu2dAQ3xb8s**. Part of the song asks the "angel baby" to never leave. The lyrics and music calmed Sean—every time I sang it to him.

Now, fast forward past the date of Sean's transition. My good friend Meryl sent me a photo of the radio screen in her car. "Angel Baby" was playing. She knew I'd sung it to Sean and needed to show it to me. I had not heard the song in years, but she heard it on the radio many more times. I believe Sean was doing his best to let me know that he was still, and always would be, my angel baby.

***

Sean's signs were coming through to me, as well as to his sister. Shannon and I discussed how we could honor Sean in a very personal way. We both decided to get matching tattoos on the insides of our right ring fingers that said: "Lava you." Sean would rarely say, "Love you." He always said, "Lava you," or often just,

"Lavaaaaaa," to Shannon. Shannon found a wonderful place in Venice, California, Black Diamond Tattoo. I made plans to meet her there.

On the flight, I sat next to a couple of young women who asked the reason for my trip. During our conversation, I learned that one of them had just lost her brother. My heart went out to her and we talked all through the flight about our loved ones who'd transitioned. I told her I was going to get a tattoo and shared the "Lava you" story. I gave her my business card, and said that if she ever needed to talk, to give me a call. Her grief was raw, and I could relate to her pain and anguish.

At Black Diamond Tattoo, Shannon and I were grateful that the respectful staff put us in a private room for the process. The tears we shed were not from the pain of the needle, but from the holes each of us had in our hearts. Shannon said she missed "Boy," her nickname for Sean, but we knew, and felt, he was right there with us as we had those precious words inked into our skin.

After receiving our tattoos, Shannon and I went to a rooftop lounge overlooking the Pacific Ocean and toasted Sean. It was a beautiful weekend, filled with

Tattoos in honor of Sean.

love and tears. Now, every time I look down to touch his fingerprint on my ring, I see "Lava you" tattooed on that finger.

The irony is that I had told Sean, "Don't ever get a tattoo. They look tacky." I know he is laughing because I now have two tattoos honoring Sean. The other one I have is of an elephant with a heart at the end of its trunk. Sean and I share a bond with elephants and would give them as gifts to one another. They represent love, family, and devotion, even after physical death. An elephant will continually visit the death site of a loved one long afterwards. It's been said that elephants never forget.

After I got the elephant tattoo, I was cleaning out drawers and closets and came across the shirt that Sean was dressed in when we brought him home after he was born. It was that of an elephant mama holding her baby with a heart at the trunk. It was very similar to the picture of the tattoo on my ankle. Another synchronicity! I had that shirt framed, and it hangs on my bedroom wall.

My love for Sean will endure forever.

***

Months after I'd gotten the first tattoo, there was a short movie released by Pixar for children about a singing volcano. Of course, the lyrics involve what volcanoes produce—lava.

Sean was about to get our attention again.

I received a text from an unknown number: "Hi Linda. I don't know if you remember me, but we met on the plane going to L.A. I remembered the story you told me about your son and the reason you had 'Lava you' tattooed on your finger. I was babysitting today, and the kids were watching this movie about a volcano that was singing, 'I lava you,' and I knew this message was for you. I hope you are doing okay."

I sent that text to Shannon, and she told me that one of her friends had just told her that she needed to watch that same film. She had trouble locating it, but when she did, she understood the importance of the message. (The film is titled "Lava" and here is a link to the song: www.youtube.com/watch?v=uh4dTLJ9q9o.)

Because of these signs, I truly felt it was Sean letting us know that he loved us, and that he approved of our new tattoos. I remembered the words of my long-ago friend's conversation: "They will use any means necessary to get the message across to you." I would have never even been aware of this movie; movies from the Pixar studios never came into my field of attention. Sean was certainly using "any means."

CHAPTER 5

Running: Not Away, But Towards

When we have concluded our journey...our body shall be returned to Earth. Our Spirit will walk amidst the clouds, and our Soul will travel again among the stars.
~ Violet Aura

In order to keep my mind from incessantly reviewing the events of the last few months after Sean's transition, the act of running became by sanctuary. I have been a runner my whole life. I'd practiced it as an exercise, and as an active meditation. Now it was more than those activities—it was saving my sanity.

Running was a way to release my emotions, if only for an hour. The beauty of the desert, along with the hawks and owls, accompanied me on each run. Those birds of prey flew in majestic patterns in the sky. A gorgeous white owl would sit on different light poles and turn his agile head as I ran by. I often wondered if he were watching over me. As the sun set, the sky would change from a beautiful shade of turquoise to red, then pink, and finally give way to darkness. On cue, I would hear the coyotes howling, beginning their call to hunt. It all transported me to another place, and I didn't have to think about my life, even if only for a little while.

And there were feathers. Many, many feathers.

While running, I'd see copious amounts of feathers. There were big ones, small ones, as well as multi-colored ones. I'd been running in the same area for many years but would never find feathers—especially large feathers—anywhere. Now there were feathers everywhere—standing straight up in the rocks, others were lying in my path. I'd stop, collect each one, and say thanks to the spiritual realm. Feathers are one of the ways that spirit lets us know they are near, like a friendly hello from those who are in the non-physical.

Even when I was not running, I noticed that big white feathers would show up on top of Sean's car. I kept every single one with heartfelt thanks and love. I was so excited to receive those feathers that I couldn't wait to see what else his spirit would show me as a sign. I didn't have to wait too long.

It was a perfect fall evening. There wasn't a cloud in the sky and the temperature was ideal for running—cool enough to feel a slight chill when the breeze blew through. The beautiful Arizona sunset was just beginning to take shape. The colors were shades of robin's egg blue, and the horizon seemed endless. There were hot air balloons dotting the sky. It looked more like a postcard than reality.

As I headed out for a run, I felt the urge to look back at my house. Right over the roof was one of the most beautiful rainbows I have ever seen. At first, I marveled at the vivid colors of purple, blue, and various shades of red. Then it occurred to me—how could there be a rainbow without clouds, without moisture in the air? I looked everywhere to see if there was a random cloud somewhere that could have produced the spectacular colors. There was not one cloud in sight, not even a tiny one.

Then I remembered reading that one of the ways to connect with someone on the other side is to imagine a rainbow from your heart to theirs. Tears began to flow. My heart and Sean's heart—our hearts were connecting. I collected myself, and started the run with my partner, my Husky, a beautiful dog named Banshee. It felt as if my feet weren't even touching the ground. I thanked Sean, and all my loved ones who had crossed over, for their incredible love and support. I needed it now more than ever.

The longer I ran, the more doubt began to rear its ugly head. I said aloud to Sean, "If that was you, thank you for the beautiful message. I miss you so much. I wish I could talk to you if only to say 'hi,' but I am grateful…truly I am."

Once again, tears streamed down my face and dripped onto my shirt. Did I want a message—any message—so much that I was able to imagine them? How could that happen, when I wasn't even thinking about a rainbow? There was a battle going on between my logical, linear brain, and my intuitive, expansive heart.

The path I run in this community includes a wide variety of cacti, as well as trees and beautiful bushes that bloom throughout the year. One particular day, the bushes were exploding in shades of pink and white, and the scent was lovely. As I passed an area behind a wall where there was a path to a house, out of nowhere, a little boy with blonde hair who resembled Sean as a child popped up from behind

Perfectly shaped heart cloud in front of our home.

a bush as if he had been hiding. "Hi," he said. I had earbuds in, so I pulled them off to hear him as I stopped running, thinking perhaps he might be lost. Again, he said, "Hi." Then he waved, giggled, and ran toward the house on the other side of the wall. I don't know if that was a hello from Sean, but I can tell you that my heart was happy. I have run that path many times since, and never saw that little blonde cutie ever again.

Another incredible sign was a cloud, but not just any cloud. Once again, I was headed out to exercise, this time for a bike ride. I went inside the house to retrieve my phone—I never ride without it and had left it on the counter. I always ask for a sign when I am outside, and this one was, as my aunt Louise would say, "a doozy!" There, right in front of the house, was a perfectly shaped heart cloud. Not one that you could possibly interpret as a heart, but without a doubt, an exact heart shaped cloud. As I rode my bike, I followed the cloud until it dissipated into the sky. My heart was soaring with love for Sean and my family in spirit.

Another day, as I was watering plants in our front yard, a hummingbird hovered close to my left ear. Its wing motion was so loud that it sounded like a giant mosquito. When I turned to face it, I assumed it would fly away. It didn't. It stayed right next to me for what seemed like a full minute before landing on a flower.

It was the first time in my memory that a hummingbird was socially interactive with me. In fact, I rarely noticed them as they drank nectar from flowers—not to linger around me, or any other human, who happened to be nearby.

After that experience, I'd encounter hummingbirds wherever I went. Some have even landed near me, to just hang out for a while. I marvel at their agility and beautiful colors. I researched the meaning of this sign and discovered that birds and insects show up to say 'hello' from a loved one, and I believe it is true.

On a run with Banshee a few weeks later, I noticed a dove sitting on the sidewalk ahead of us. It was near the grass, and I thought as soon as we approached, it would fly away. Birds are prey for Huskies and Banshee has been known to leap in the air to catch one in mid-flight. As we approached the bird, it remained in place. I thought perhaps it was hurt, so I ran around it.

Beloved running partner, and best buddy, Banshee, 2005-2019.

Banshee never saw the dove, even though it was directly to the left of him, clearly in his line of sight. I thought it was odd that he never saw it. His vision was quite acute, especially when it involved catching a feathered snack before dinner.

We made a turn on our route that took us back by the dove's location. This time it was directly in front of Banshee. I thought that surely he'd see it. I was nervous for the little bird, and gripped Banshee's leash with all my strength, ready to hold him back, knowing he would do whatever he could to get a taste of the dove. He ran right by, never noticing it. The dove turned its head to watch us. When Banshee and I were about 30 feet away, I looked back to see the little bird take flight.

What do I think it meant? Maybe it was not a sign from Sean, but another important message for me—from the natural world. A dove is a sign of peace, and I'd been praying for inner peace. Peace reigned in that moment between me, the dove, and my dog. I thanked spirit for the message.

Sean's car even gave me a sign. When he'd driven it, it always smelled of artificial pine. That disgusting scent was so strong I had to roll the windows down when I was his passenger. I remember telling him to stop buying those hanging green trees because they were full of chemicals, but he just laughed.

Why is this relevant? In the first year of grief, I'd only looked at his car with heartache and memories. It stayed in the garage most of the time and was only driven occasionally by his dad to keep the battery charged and the engine operational.

A year later, I decided it was time for me to drive his car to continue my healing process. I knew the cardboard tree air freshener was in the glove compartment, and after locating it, I was glad the smell had dissipated and happy to dispose of it. Yet, off and on for about six months afterwards, when I'd drive his car, a pine scent that came from some unseen place would overwhelm me. I knew it was Sean was letting me know he was with me, getting the last laugh. With a smile on my face, I'd happily roll down the window until the smell subsided and thank him for a sign that I'd hoped was free of chemicals.

On a related note, occasionally I'll get a whiff of his cologne or smell a cigar while sitting alone in our backyard. Sean liked a cigar now and then, so I believe it's his way of saying "Hi mom. What's new with you?"

The messages became more frequent. I honestly don't know how I would have survived without them, and thanked spirit every day. They were the balm for my aching soul, but I longed for something more. I missed seeing Sean's handsome face and gorgeous smile.

Wanting to continue my healing, instead of waiting for signs, I decided to take some action.

CHAPTER 6

A Leave of Presence

Death ends a life, not a relationship.
~ Jack Lemmon

Shannon told me about a sacred place that she'd visited near the Joshua Tree National Park—the Integratron. It is a dome-shaped building, built for sound healing events. It is filled with mementos of love and gratitude from people all over the world. Shannon had gone with her boyfriend, Eddie, before their marriage, and each had experienced tones that filled the room with different frequencies.

During the sound healing they experienced, Eddie fell into a deep sleep. Shannon found it difficult to wake him, and she had to shake him several times before he came back to a state of awareness. Shannon's experience was different. She could see the wood panels, and the flowers inside the dome, emanating energy. It was unlike anything she had ever experienced.

I wondered what might occur with me if I were to experience sound healing inside the Integratron. Shannon and I planned a mother-daughter trip that October. I was excited about what I might encounter.

Before we arrived at the Integratron, I asked Sean to let us know he was around. I wasn't expecting anything immediately, but a few minutes later, my cell phone rang. These were the numbers on the screen: 000-000-0000. I picked up the call only to hear static on the line, like a call from a long distance, with bad reception.

As we drove down the dirt road to unlock the chain link fence that separates the property from the street, I noticed that the silhouette of the Integratron's building resembled a spaceship. We parked the car in a dusty parking lot nearby and waited with anticipation inside the gift shop until someone came to escort us to the dome.

As we entered the Integratron on the ground level, we noticed pictures and pages of its history on every wall. We worked our way around the building's first floor until we reached a wooden ladder. We removed our shoes and climbed up the ladder to the room where the sound healing was to take place.

Scattered on the shiny wood floor were a variety of Native American rugs. We were instructed to pick one or two to use during the ceremony. It was difficult to choose which one I wanted, because they were all so lovely. I resonated with one that had turquoise and pink tones in it, since it reminded me of the Arizona sunset. In front of us were beautiful crystal singing bowls, of all different shapes and sizes. We choose our blankets, laid down and got comfortable. Since this was a private session, we had the whole room to ourselves.

The meditation began with deep breathing, and as the singing bowls captivated us with their melodic tones, I felt as if I was slipping out of my body. I know this concept is strange to those who have never heard of or who have had an Out of Body Experience (OBE), but that is exactly how I felt. I dropped the heaviness of my physical body and began, for lack of a better word, traveling effortlessly around the room. It was as if I was looking down over everything in that space. I wasn't scared, I just had a sense of freedom that I had never felt before. I remember thinking, "What an amazing experience, but now what?"

At one point, before I came back into my body and as I was scanning the area, right in front of me was Sean's handsome face with a big smile. It was sudden and unexpected. I smiled back and reached out to touch him, but before I knew it, it was over, and he was gone. I'd received my wish. The memory of that vision is still vivid today.

The singing bowls ended, and as the Native American music permeated the air, I felt a jolt in my body. It reminded me of the TV medical shows when a defibrillator shocks a body to revive it during a heart attack. The density of my body was immense. I tried to move my hands, but they wouldn't budge, so I moved only my fingers. It was a slow process to return to my body, and it took quite a lot of effort. Acclimating back into the physical world was more challenging that I ever imagined.

After Shannon and I completed our session, we both said it felt strange to be 'back.' Our perceptions changed; things looked and felt different to us. It was as if we were navigating a new landscape, and we weren't sure of our surroundings. We just sat there for a while until we had our bearings again.

We were supposed to go back to the ladder and climb down. Instead, we were drawn to a hole in the middle of the room where we were told the vortex of energy was located. The hole went all the way down into the ground. I placed my hand over it and felt some sort of power coming from the space. It was a force pushing back against my hand and I could 'see' the energy. It felt deep appreciation for the Earth's power from that vortex. I will always remember the experience.

***

To get back to 'normal' we decided to take a drive around Palm Springs and see homes of celebrities such as Bob Hope and Bing Crosby—the places they used to reside in as a reprieve from the craziness of Hollywood. It was fun, and we were able to check off several addresses on our list. We drove with no particular plan or route to follow as we admired the architecture.

Then, we turned onto Rose Avenue. Rose was the name of my beloved grandmother. Perhaps not a sign, but it was a beautiful reminder of her.

Next, we found ourselves on a street named Ruth. Ruth was the name of my mother, and like my grandmother, she too was in the spirit realm. Again, cool but…probably not a sign.

We drove up and down a few other streets until Shannon turned onto a street named Archibald—the name of my dad. Seriously?

Last, but not least, as we drove to the center of town, we realized we were on a street named Alejo—the same name of my grandfather who'd died years before I was born!

Shannon and I looked at each other in astonishment. What were the chances that, without a map, we'd encounter all four streets with the names of my deceased parents and grandparents? I knew without a doubt that this was my loved ones letting us know they were with us as we honored and celebrated Sean's life. Once I realized there were so many signs, I made a practice of writing down all the synchronicities that were occurring in my, and in my family members' lives, around Sean's transition. There were so many, and I didn't want to forget any of these precious greetings from spirit.

***

That night for dinner, we walked into a random restaurant to see if a table was available. While we were waiting, a song came over the speakers. We both looked at each other and started laughing. It was Neil Diamond singing "Sweet

Caroline." The song was a favorite of Sean's—he loved to yell out the "so good" lyrics of the chorus. When that part of the song came on, everyone in the bar sang it out. Loud! I could feel tears of joy and sadness welling up inside me…joy that he let us know he was close, and sad that he wasn't there physically to sing it out with everyone else.

***

The following evening as we searched for a place to have dinner, Shannon mentioned the name of a restaurant that was very popular. So much so, that reservations were required weeks, or months, in advance. Undaunted, we decided to see if by chance a table was available. We thought it would be lucky to get a table inside because outside seating would be an impossible feat without a reservation. We asked the hostess if we could get a table and she said, "Something outside just became available. Would you like it?"

We beamed and, of course, said, "Yes." Under my breath, I thanked Sean. He was making sure we were taken care of, just like he'd done so many times before. The table we were given wasn't just any table; it was one of two with shrubbery surrounding it for privacy. The other table was reserved for the actress Suzanne Sommers. She arrived about 30 minutes later with a group of friends and her laughter permeated the beautiful secluded dining area.

It was a magical evening as we talked about our weekend in Palm Springs with one another and our shared deep love for Sean.

CHAPTER 7
A Sister Speaks as She is Spoken To

Death takes the body. God takes the soul. Our mind holds the memories. Our heart keeps the love. Our faith lets us know we will meet again.
~ Anonymous

Sean had met Shannon's boyfriend Eddie before he left for deployment. At that time, Sean called to tell me that he liked him and thought Eddie was a good guy. Sean was always very protective of us. He would have let Shannon know if he didn't approve of her choice. This type of protection happened after Sean transitioned, too.

I asked Shannon if she would write something about her experiences with Sean in spirit. Here, she shares perspectives on life with Sean and encounters with his spirit.

Sean and I were just 18 months apart, and we had a strong sibling bond. Of course, in our childhood we never wanted to say, "I love you." It seemed too mushy, so we turned that saying into "olive juice," which later became "lava you" and sometimes just an exaggerated "lavaaaaa."

Since Sean passed, I've had my fair share of occurrences that could be chalked up to nothing more than a strange coincidence. For example, I see repeating numbers every day. Usually it's 11:11, but it can also be 1:11, 2:22, and so forth. It's not always just on a clock, either; it could be the mileage on my car, the number of calories I've burned when I glance down at the treadmill, or the number of seconds left on the microwave. But it happens every single day, without fail, often multiple times throughout the day.

Unusual phone calls have come to my telephone on more than one occasion. A week or so after Sean passed, I was lying on the couch with my then-boyfriend (now husband). It was about 11 at night. His phone rang. Startled, we looked at the caller ID. There was no name, and it was not even a real telephone number: 0000000000. We looked at each other, and then he answered. There was no response to his "hello." Just static.

White feathers sometimes pop up in places they shouldn't be. One afternoon I was holding my infant son inside our house, by the storm door made of glass. It was winter and snow was falling, and I wanted my baby to see it. Out of nowhere, inside the house, a small white feather drifted down in front of my face and landed at my feet. Confused, I looked around to find the source and then looked at my son, as if he might somehow have an answer.

The most striking events were when my friends reached out to me with messages from or dreams about Sean. Some of these friends were people who I hadn't spoken to in years. The timing of these communications usually happens around some kind of significant event in my life. Here are a few examples:

I had my 30th birthday one year after Sean passed. My friend Marisa, who I hadn't seen in months, called and left a voicemail. To my surprise, she wished me happy birthday and insisted I watch a short film that she emailed to me. She had gone to see a Pixar movie, and had also seen an animated short film. The file in her email was corrupt. I deleted the link, figured I would watch it eventually, but forgot about it.

Later that evening, Marisa contacted my husband. She asked him to find a working version of the link so I could watch it. After a few minutes of searching, we found a link that worked and watched the short film titled "Lava."

The week before my wedding, I received a message from my friend Julia, who grew up with us and knew Sean. Julia is a very pragmatic person, and she is someone who I turn to when I don't want sugar-coated advice. She doesn't believe in anything extraordinary that could be proven otherwise with facts or reason. This was her message: "So two nights ago I had THE most vivid dream about Sean. I'm not sure I've ever dreamt of him since he passed (or at all for that matter. Then, right as I was dreaming, I was wakened by my closet light going on. Just out of thin air, it popped on. It's never done that before and it's entirely inexplicable for a variety of reasons...it's definitely not on a timer or anything like that. I definitely turned it off before going to bed because I cannot sleep with even the slightest light in the bedroom. And Tyler [her husband] and the hound were sound asleep. I'm not 100 percent sure I 'fall' for things like this. So, I ignored it all day yesterday and this morning. And then I thought, what *if* it really was Sean trying to send me a message this week, of all weeks, that he's here with us! If that's the case, I MUST bother Shannon at the height of her busiest-ness and tell her."

A high school friend, also named Shannon, who I hadn't spoken to in over a decade, sent me a Facebook message. Since we'd lost touch after high school, we weren't even connected on Facebook, so she had to seek out my profile to send me a private message. She too let me know that she'd had an incredibly vivid dream about Sean, who she'd known well when they'd played on the tennis team together in school. She apologized for reaching out so randomly, but said she felt a strong urge that she needed to get in touch with me after having this dream: "Hey I'm sorry if this is weird and out of left field. I had the most vivid dream about your brother two nights ago and I can't get it out of my head. But at the end of it, he said, "You've always been my second favorite Shannon." I thought sending you this might be strange, but I just can't shake the feeling that I wanted to share it. It was just probably the most real feeling dream I've ever had. Anyway, I hope life finds you well and I really just wanted to share with you that I was thinking of him."

Shannon's accounts are important because she usually chalks up these events as coincidences. However, when she shared her experiences with me, I knew that they meant something extraordinary to her.

I learned that Eddie had also received the unusual phone call with all the zeros on the caller ID call just as I had. Neither one of us has ever received another one. Was it a call from the other side of the veil to say, "Lava you?"

***

Later, I discovered scientists have long used mathematics to describe the physical properties of the universe. Was this the way the universe could communicate with us in terms that we could understand? I too see repeating numbers all the time, and no longer question if they are a coincidence.

CHAPTER 8
The Message is the Medium

Life does not end when we die. Death is a rebirth into a spirit world of light and love, a transition from the physical to the spiritual that is no more frightening or painful than passing between rooms through an open doorway. It is a joyful homecoming to our natural home.
~ Betty Eadie

Before Sean passed, I had never spoken to an evidential medium. By "evidential," I mean a person who receives messages from spirit and has been tested to show that he or she is capable of sharing evidence that's important only for the sitter. The sitter is the person seeking messages from the realm beyond Earth.

I heard about Michelle Beltran through a friend. Michelle had worked as a police officer and with detectives on certain cases, so I knew she had outstanding credentials. By email, I set up a date for a phone session with her a few weeks after Sean transitioned. My head was still in a fog, and I hoped to get some validation from her that he was safe and happy.

That was all I truly wanted to know at that time. Michelle asked that I tell her nothing until we spoke. She also said to just answer 'yes' or 'no' to validate the response. I was both nervous and excited that I might hear from Sean through her.

When the session began, we said a prayer together, and then she asked me if I had a son in spirit.

"Yes." Even saying that seemed surreal.

"He just recently crossed over, and is resting," she said, "but I can also feel part of his energy here with me. You see, energy can be in many places at once; not like us who are bound by physical laws."

She said he was very strong, his passing was sudden and unexpected, and it had taken him by complete surprise. He wanted her to let me know that he was fine, and safe now.

Perhaps that was the case, but it is too vague. Not exactly what I'd hoped for. What else would she tell me to ease my mind?

She said, "Your son said you don't believe what I am saying, and he is laughing."

I was taken aback. Was she a mind reader instead of a medium? I thought I'd better be more careful about what I was thinking!

Michelle shared that on his father's birthday, Sean had been with him. He knew it was a difficult day. At the time, we were planning Sean's funeral service instead of celebrating.

Then Sean delivered the message that he was OK with his sister moving in with her boyfriend.

"Wait. What?" I thought. "Moving in with her boyfriend?" She'd never mentioned that to me. I knew my next phone call after Michelle would be to Shannon, but it was true that Kevin's birthday occurred the week we were planning Sean's service. I wasn't sure about Shannon moving in with Eddie.

Michelle said that Sean would be letting us know he was around after he was rested. She told me to listen for beeps, like a truck backing up, because that would be Sean.

I laughed because it made no sense to me. A beep? Seriously? But then, as we were about to hang up, I heard a truck outside, and it was beeping as it was backing up. The reason this is so relevant is because they were paving our street that day, and no traffic was allowed on it. At that precise moment, a truck came to collect the cones, and was backing up in front of my house.

Michele said, "I hear beeping," and she laughed with me. "Don't doubt spirit," she said in a motherly tone. I could almost feel her shaking her finger at me.

This call lasted only 30 minutes. There wasn't time to ask all the questions I had, but I was relieved to have confirmation that Sean's energy was present for both Michelle and me.

I then called Shannon, told her about the reading, and said, "Michelle mentioned that you and Eddie would be moving in together."

Shannon was silent.

"Hello, are you there?" I asked, thinking the call had dropped.

"How did you know that?" Shannon asked. "We just talked about it last night, and no one knows."

I told her that Sean was tattling on her like he did when he was a kid. How was that for validation?

CHAPTER 9
Being My Own Medium... and a Metaphysician

Of course you don't die. Nobody dies. Death doesn't exist. You only reach a new level of vision, a new realm of consciousness, a new unknown world.
~ Henry Miller

Sean.

I kept seeing him, or what I thought was him, in different places.

With a doctorate degree in metaphysical counseling, I also worked as a board-certified life strategies coach, but I wondered if I was also becoming my own medium.

When Sean's belongings finally arrived a couple of months after his transition, each box held a treasure trove of mementos. Pictures, items that meant a lot to Sean, and of course his military uniforms and clothes. I would hold his shirts up to my face hug them tight. Then I'd fold each one and put it back in his dresser. Many of his possessions remained in storage for a year, and then we began donating them. I could sense that Sean was right there with me as I opened each box. The energy of love was palpable and made unpacking bearable.

***

I went back to work only a few weeks after Sean's funeral service. As a counselor, I am trained to compartmentalize my personal life from my work. I thought that listening and helping others would be the best way to get out of my head, if only for the workday.

The first morning on my way back to my office, as I pulled up to the stoplight right before turning onto the street, not one, but two U-Haul trucks pulled up alongside me. One said Annapolis, Maryland, and the other, San Diego, California. Shannon and Sean grew up in Annapolis, Maryland. Sean's last duty station was San Diego. In fact, he wanted to buy a rental unit to lease until he could move there as a permanent resident. As strange as it sounds, I felt like the trucks were giving me a big hug and telling me "You've got this, mom."

***

One evening, I was waiting in the car to pick up dinner. I still couldn't dine in public and faking polite conversation with strangers was not something I could stomach. In truth, it was all I could do to keep food down. Seeing people happy and laughing made me feel worse.

It was close to dusk, and young man walked by my car, looked at me, and smiled. For a moment, I thought he looked just like Sean and I almost jumped out of the car. Later, when I did some research on sightings, I found this example was a common occurrence. Evidently, loved ones in spirit can superimpose their face onto someone else for a brief second or two. Since then, I've heard from people who have seen visions like that of a mom, a great aunt, a grandfather, and a cousin—all deceased. At least I knew I wasn't alone. Perhaps it was just the grief talking, or seeing, but either way, it was comforting.

***

Sean's godmother Kathy told me she was at the gym and looked up. There was a college kid who looked just like Sean wearing a Hokie Bird shirt. The Hokie Bird is the mascot for Virginia Tech, his alma mater. When she glanced at the young man again, his face looked completely different—and very unlike Sean's face.

***

I kept hearing the phrase, "Pay attention." I thought I had better listen. I wasn't looking for signs; they somehow found me. Here is another good example: On a trip to the grocery store, I was driving around the parking lot. I realized I was going in the wrong direction and made a U-turn. As I turned, I saw a Jeep Cherokee Limited with a license plate that read USN 0206. I stopped the car and just stared at it.

Meaningful sign from spirit.

Sean's birthday is February 6—there's the 0206—and the U.S. Navy is represented by the USN. I took a picture of the license plate because I needed proof to show others. Sean loved our family's Jeep Cherokee Limited. We'd had it for over 20 years, and he drove it until it fell apart. But now I had a photo to show to everyone who knew this fact about us and Sean, and I was happy that I took the picture because I thought I'd never see that Jeep again.

Spirit had other ideas. Living in a gated community, access is limited. As I pulled out of the community onto the main street to go out of the gate later that day, the same Jeep pulled in front of me. It was as if Sean was validating that he was always here. How cool is that? The phrase, "Pay attention," was now making complete sense to me.

***

Holidays, especially the first ones after a loved one transitions into spirit, are challenging. We had invited Sean's godmother, Kathy, and Shannon, for Thanksgiving. Kathy had been a rock of solid support for me during the first few months after Sean's transition to spirit. She called me every day, and if all I could do was cry, she listened. I'll be forever grateful for her love and support. More than a sister-in-law to me, Kathy is a sister in every sense of the word.

Kathy gifted me with a beautiful set of wine glasses, each with an etched dragonfly design. Thanksgiving seemed like the perfect occasion to use them. As we clinked our glasses in a toast to Sean, while watching the sunset, I heard what sounded like glass shattering. I looked around and said, "Did anyone else hear that?"

Everyone shook their heads yes. We ran into the house to see what had broken. I was afraid Banshee would step on the glass, so I wanted to make sure to clean it up. We looked everywhere…and found nothing. None of us could explain where the sound came from, but we'd all clearly heard glass shattering.

That evening as we were finishing the dishes, I realized one of the wine glasses was missing. There had been one left hanging in the wine cabinet. I looked everywhere but couldn't find it. I thought maybe someone had inadvertently put it in the wrong cupboard, but it was gone. I looked everywhere trying to find the glass, but never did locate it. This was yet another strange event that cannot be explained using logic.

***

The more often these kinds of occurrences happened, my research also increased. I learned that as a spirit gets stronger energetically, it is able to communicate more easily, especially in the first year after passing. That is the time when their loved ones need comforting the most—while being in deep states of grief and sadness.

Electricity seems to be a good vehicle for communication by spirits. Quantum physics holds that everything has a field of energy, from rocks to human beings, and electricity is an easy medium for them to use.

Shannon had an unexplained event with the electricity in her apartment. For an unknown reason, some of her lights kept going off and on. She thought there might be a short in the wiring and called an electrician to solve the problem. He couldn't find anything wrong, and the lights appeared to be working fine when he was there. She thought it was a fluke. However, one particular morning, she was running late for work. The light in her bathroom went out, so she said, "Sean, I am going to be late for work. If this is you, turn the light back on!" It came on.

I told Kevin that story and he just smiled. He doesn't share the same beliefs that I do about the afterlife. However, shortly after that incident, the middle light over my vanity went out. Not uncommon, but I thought of Shannon and said, "Sean, if this is you, turn it back on." It came on. Kevin was in the room, and the middle light on the opposite side of the sink went out. He said, "Let's see if it comes back on." It did. I know he didn't believe it was something other than a fluke or a coincidence.

So many of these kinds of events were happening that I couldn't just brush them off. Sean's energy was strong, and I felt that he was working hard to prove it to us.

Here is yet another incident (involving technology) that can't be explained. A family member was attempting to buy something on an online shopping site. It was set up with an automatic login so he could bypass the password. Every time he attempted to log in, the site would give an error message: "Invalid password." This didn't make sense to him, so after a couple of attempts, he went to an encrypted spreadsheet to see what password he had used.

There, in black and white, was the password "Sean&Pop!" Definitely not encrypted! Pop is the nickname Sean used for his dad.

When I was told about it, I replied, "Do you think a dead person could do that?" I am not sure why that response came flying out of my mouth so quickly, but it did. It even shocked me! To this day, I still have no logical explanation how that could have occurred, but in my heart, I know who changed the password!

***

My need for constant study took me to the Afterlife Research and Education Institute's (AREI) conference in Scottsdale in 2015. One of the speakers was an evidential medium named Susanne Wilson. Susanne worked in the corporate world for many years, although from childhood she could sense spirit. This ability blossomed after she had a near death experience in a doctor's office while being tested for allergies. She experienced an anaphylactic reaction—her throat swelled to a point where she could no longer breathe. She left her body and looked down at the nurse and doctor who were trying to resuscitate her; she was unafraid and curious. With what she describes as a "whoosh," she came back into her body.

I knew that soon after the AREI conference Susanne was scheduled to speak at an event at a bookstore in Scottsdale. I signed up to attend. Susanne said she would give some readings to just a few people in the group, so I surrendered to spirit, as she had requested. I watched with anticipation as she picked up a pad of paper and began scribbling on it. She looked right at me, pointed, and said, "Do you have a son in spirit?"

"Yes." I could feel my whole body begin to tremble with excitement.

"Please stand. He has a message for you."

I was hoping to hear from Sean but wasn't sure if I was the only one in the room who fit the description. Susanne said, "First let me make sure that I have the right person. Was your son in the military? I see a white Navy uniform and he is saluting me."

"Yes," I said.

Then she asked, "Did he just make the rank of lieutenant? I am seeing lieutenant bars on his uniform."

"He achieved the rank of lieutenant in May of 2014."

I wasn't prepared for what she told me next. "He's saying he went on deployment, and he took the book you'd given him. He says, 'Mom, I hope you don't mind but I gave that book to a person who needed it more than I did.'"

There is no way Susanne could have known about that book. It was one authored by Louise Hay, and I hadn't even told my family that I'd given it to him.

Susanne went on: "Now he is thanking you for the rest of the goodies you gave him, including a salt block tea light holder."

Again, I marveled at how she could know such private information, including some that I had forgotten.

When Susanne said that Sean wanted me to know I'd be writing a book, I shook my head "no." I could barely get through the day with work and family issues to take care of, much less concentrate on writing a book.

She saw me shake my head and said: "He said, 'Not now, but it's coming.'"

Susanne knew things that only Sean and I would understand. My heart was beating out of my chest, and it felt like my feet weren't touching the ground.

Having that reading brought me great relief.

But still…I needed more.

CHAPTER 10
Research for Comfort

Oh wow, oh wow, oh wow.
~ Steve Jobs (his final words)

The first year following Sean's passing, I spent a lot of time and energy attempting to convince family and friends that consciousness survives death. I wanted them to know about all the evidence and information that I had spent hundreds of hours researching so they too would know there was validity to the work I had done. It was fruitless. My frustration was growing exponentially. No one seemed to want to hear what I was saying. I was met with opposition, apathy, rolling eyes, and shaking heads. I was constantly experiencing the fearful rejection of people even when they were presented with credible and evidential data.

Looking back, I now understand that everyone has a right to their own beliefs. Who was I to try to convince them otherwise? I knew my experiences were valid, and that was all the confirmation I needed. Everyone is on their own spiritual path, and instead of getting frustrated, I needed to step back and honor where they were on their own sacred journey. Perhaps the amnesic state which keeps many from understanding the instinctive knowing that everyone is born with is a symptom of our society's fear of dying.

Still, I dived even deeper into every scientific piece of literature I could find on afterlife topics. I downloaded at least 80 books written by doctors, skeptics, lawyers, scientists, philosophers, and researchers who had spent years documenting the survival of consciousness. I couldn't understand why the traditional scientific and religious dogmatic communities refused to accept, or even look at the data. I felt they needed to release their incessant hold onto prejudices, divisions, and their own beliefs. How else could they consider the possibility of another reality, other than what they had been taught? Isn't that what science is about? Scientists are always questioning theories and probabilities. My quest for answers to the questions that had eluded me all these years, became a guiding force in my life. I began following the route of respected intellects in the field of non-linear consciousness.

After Sean crossed over in 2014, I desperately searched for some like-minded souls who could help me on my own journey. Research had taken me a great distance, but I was ready to leave the dock and explore uncharted territory.

The AREI conference in Scottsdale in 2015 was the answer to one of my many prayers. This consortium of scientists, researchers, mediums, and speakers were people who'd studied aspects of the afterlife and had done so for many years. They were the ones who continued to push the boundaries of conventional beliefs. Isn't that what science is supposed to do, and not be firmly cemented in a dogmatic belief system? I was fortunate to hear a beautiful mother named Elizabeth Boisson speak about her children in spirit and the organization she co-founded, Helping Parents Heal. She became a lifeline for me, and I'll be forever grateful for her kindness and compassion.

During this conference, I was introduced to and spoke with a number of scientists, doctors, and researchers and as we discussed the survival of consciousness, I learned the remarkable story of Eben Alexander, M.D., a neurologist who'd contracted bacterial meningitis. It had enveloped his brain, causing it to swell. I myself had suffered from viral meningitis numerous times, and the pain was so severe, even the smallest amount of light pierced my brain. My head felt like it was in a vise. Dr. Alexander had left his body and went to another reality when he was ill. He tells the story in his book, *Proof of Heaven: A Neurosurgeon's Journey into the Afterlife*.

Not long after the conference, I had the good fortune of taking an online class with Dr. Alexander. He was so incredibly knowledgeable of the brain; if anyone could dismiss that kind of experience he'd had, it would've been him. I asked him if he thought that being a neurosurgeon was one of the reasons for his out of body occurrence.

He responded, "I don't know for sure, but maybe so."

The AREI conference brought another unique experience to me. At a breakout session, I struck up a conversation with a priest. As a former Catholic, I was hoping he'd share his brand of spiritual advice and provide some words of wisdom and comfort for me. Our discussion began and ended on the topic of mediumship. In a stern tone, told me that a belief in the ability to speak with the departed was "blasphemy."

"Excuse me?" I said, shocked and dismayed. "When we are instructed in church to pray and listen for a response, whom are we speaking with? We wait in anticipation for an answer, we are told to be patient and to have faith. Someone has to be there to respond to prayers. Right?"

"Only those sanctioned by the Church have the ability to communicate," he said.

That seemed nonsensical and irrational to me. He represented the dogma ingrained into certain religious beliefs. I couldn't comprehend why this priest was at the afterlife conference.

Our conversation ceased after his response. (My hope is that his beliefs changed after the conference.)

I wondered why the Church taught that no one else could have the experiences I was having with Sean in spirit—except Jesus and maybe a chosen few? As a child I learned that Jesus was God, made in the image of man. Why then couldn't all people have this ability?

Jesus is quoted in the Bible, in John 14:12, (KJV), "Verily, verily, I say unto you, he that believeth on me, the works that I do shall he do also; and greater works than these shall he do; because I go unto my Father."

Why is it plausible to believe that Jesus rose from the dead state (a Christian belief), talked to his disciples, and then ascended into another realm, and yet we who are made in his image aren't gifted with the ability to converse with our loved ones in the spirit?

Being at the AREI conference was like taking a journey down the rabbit hole—and I felt like the character Alice when she descended into Wonderland. As I plummeted even deeper, I met more and more interesting characters. I was given pages of unpublished books, published research papers, and sites for documentary films to explore on my own time. I was grateful for each and every one.

When the conference ended, I did the homework and became an avid reader of the experts in this field. I marveled at the questions they had asked and were asking, and what they'd discovered about the existence of consciousness after the physical life no longer exists.

Why wasn't this all over the media? What were people so afraid of?

***

With every book I read, and every lecture I listened to, I became more and more confident that Sean was doing fine and thriving in another reality, and that we could absolutely communicate with each other. I felt as if I'd known the truth all along: Energy never dies. It just changes form.

Humans, according to science, are composed of 7 x 10 to the 27th power of atoms. Most atoms are 99.9999 percent made up of empty space. Atoms are vortexes of energy. The first law of thermodynamics states that energy cannot be created or destroyed, it can only change from one form to another. So, if humans are made mostly of energy and energy cannot be destroyed, where does the energetic aspect of a human go after the physical body dies?

Physicist Max Planck, Ph.D., ForMemRS, stated: "As a man who has devoted his whole life to the most clear headed science, to the study of matter, I can tell you as a result of my research about the atoms this much: There is no matter as such! All matter originates and exists only by virtue of a force which brings the particles of an atom to vibration and holds this most minute solar system of the atom together.... We must assume behind this force the existence of a conscious and intelligent Spirit. This Spirit is the matrix of all matter." (From *"Das Wesen der Materie* [The Nature of Matter]," a speech he gave in Florence, Italy in 1944. Planck received the Nobel Prize in 1918.)

I surmise that the body is only a vehicle—some call it "an Earth suit"—to house the etheric energy of the spirit and the mind's consciousness. Neuroscientists cannot locate the place of consciousness in the brain, heart, or anywhere in the physicality of the human body. In fact, no one knows exactly where consciousness-holding or -determining neurons are located, or what distinguishes them from other neurons. However, Stuart Hameroff, M.D., an anesthesiologist, and Director of the Center for Consciousness Studies at the University of Arizona, as well as British quantum physicist Sir Roger Penrose, contends that consciousness resides in a quantum state in "microtubules."

So, the debate continues. Human energy has been studied for ages by scientists…and by regular people…in their own bodies.

There is more attention now given to an ancient, yet common, belief that the body contains energy centers known as chakras. The word chakra comes from an ancient Indian language known as Sanskrit. Chakra means vortex, spinning wheel, or circle. Chakras, the major centers of spiritual power in the human body, are circles of energy that balance, store, and distribute the power of life through the physical body. Picture a glow, or aura, around the body that vibrates with this energy. That's known as the subtle body. The subtle body is the spirit, the energetic overlay of the physical body. There are other words to describe spirit energy in the body: chi in Chinese, and prana in Sanskrit. Some alternative medicine practitioners call themselves "energy healers." Allopathic, or western medicine practitioners, don't recognize chakras (or know what to do with them), even though these terms have been around for thousands of years. Is it possible that the halos crowning those represented in the Bible, were actually depictions of their own energy field? That question is still up for debate centuries later.

Lynne McTaggart wrote a brilliant book, *The Field: The Quest for the Secret Force of the Universe*, in 2008. In it, she questioned where consciousness was located. Could it be inside the body "or out there in the Field?" Her theory, after conducting thousands of experiments, was that the brain is a processor of consciousness, much like a computer has a processor, and an operating system, but it only stores and houses the information for use. It doesn't create it. When the brain dies, it is believed that the field of consciousness then leaves the body through either the solar plexus or the top of the head (the crown) and returns to the source of its energy.

Could this process involve the "microtubules" Hameroff and Penrose referenced?

If a dying—or clinically declared dead—person is resuscitated back to life, does it mean their energy of consciousness and spirit can still be downloaded back into the processor, brain, and body? The concept of a Near Death Experience (NDE) has been written about, studied, and debated since the 1975 publication of *Life After Life: The Investigation of a Phenomenon—Survival of Bodily Death*, by Raymond Moody.

In the years since Sean transitioned away from his physical, Earthly energy, I have had the good fortune to speak with a number of people who have had NDEs. The experiencers told me that they'd left their body in one of two ways: through the top of their head, or their solar plexus region. With so many people around the world having this experience, an organization called the International Association for Near Death Studies (IANDS), based in Durham, North Carolina, was founded in 1981. It is comprised of physicians, scientists, and researchers in the field of non-local consciousness.

As I spoke to each experiencer about their NDE, I wanted to know what they felt during the moment of death. Were they scared, confused, joyous? What was their experience like on the other side of the veil? Although each one was different, their recurring words reflected the themes of "beautiful" and "peaceful." They had shed their physical bodies and became free from the constraints that physicality demands.

One woman, observing her physical body below her on the ground, thought, "Oh my goodness, do I really look that old?" Even though her "temporary death" was sudden and unexpected, she remembered giggling when she realized that she was still very much alive. She was "on a high," as she described it.

One man named John said that while he was "dead," he felt better than he ever had in his physical life. Sick for a good portion of his adult life, John remembered being free from debilitating pain.

The concept of "freedom" was also a common denominator in every NDE case I'd explored with experiencers. John was surprised that he was able to be in several places at one time. This is called bilocation. In some simultaneous way, John's spirit was with his wife and daughter who were at his hospital bedside, and also with the rest of his family who were out in the waiting room.

These conversations alleviated some or most of the fear that I had with Sean's passing. I had asked myself many times if he was scared, fearful, or if the moment of passing was peaceful. Hearing the experiences of others, trusting them, and believing that Sean had a similar experience, calmed my anxiety.

Many who had NDEs related to car accidents or sudden and unexpected deaths said that their spirit left their body moments before the event happened. Many described watching the accident or health crisis as it happened. Of course, I cannot verify these experiences, but having sensed the consistency they've provided, who am I to say it doesn't occur? I only know that having these conversations was another steppingstone along my journey to explore the survival of consciousness.

What I could not know at the time I sought and gathered this information was that I too would soon have my own NDE.

CHAPTER 11
Self-Science

This wallpaper is dreadful. One of us will have to go.
~ Oscar Wilde

The experience that I define as mystical, or transpersonal, may have been an NDE—or an Out of Body Experience (OBE). I'm still not sure. To me, these terms are not as relevant as the experience was because I will remember it forever.

I had just finished a kickboxing routine and a shower before I headed outdoors to enjoy beverages and snacks with Kevin. Over that Easter weekend, a lunar eclipse was to occur, and I'd looked forward to observing it. As I sat down, suddenly my toes began to curl. They were cramping. Then my fingers mimicked my toes. Because of the intense exercise, I knew my body was probably low in potassium, magnesium and sodium. I mentioned that I should probably be eating a banana, but we were enjoying other appetizers. I forgot about it and eventually the cramping dissipated.

Later that evening, I was relaxing on the couch, settling in for the night, and engaging in conversation in our family room when something strange happened. I blinked and suddenly realized that I was no longer in my physical body.

I was somewhere else, but where? My heart didn't stop beating, but I had disengaged from life, free from any physical constraints of the world. A beautiful white light surrounded me. Even though it appeared to be brighter than the sun, my eyes were magnetically drawn to it. I became one with the light.

Inside the light was my beloved dad. He had a big smile on his face that assured me I would be OK. I couldn't get close enough to touch him, but I was so happy, I couldn't stop smiling. He looked younger and had more hair than he did in the few black-and-white photos I still had of him. I could feel the warmth of the light, full of love as I stood there, just as I had when we were together driving the car, and I was a happy 4-year-old. I was awed by the emergence of my dad's physical form into my awareness. A sea of consciousness flowed all around me, pulsating with life.

Then, I felt the need to look down to see my 'other' self. Was I taller? What was I wearing? Was I still in pajamas? To my surprise, unlike my dad who was fully attired, I was a beam of pure white light—like I was wearing a glimmering gown made only of sparking light beams.

This was profound. While dressed in that gown of light, I could see with my eyes, hear with my ears, and speak, although I don't recall saying anything. It was all thought. I was communicating through telepathy. I felt physical, but there was nothing physical about me in that gown. I felt safe, like I was home again and ready to stay. There was such an intense feeling of the aura of love and peace—feelings that are difficult to articulate in our limited language. One thing I could give credence to, was that the light that surrounded me was conscious, and loving. It encircled me with pure, unadulterated joy. There was no separation between me and the light. Even though I was without a physical anatomy, I was alive in every sense of the word. Death was nothing more than an expansion of some vast consciousness. Of that, I was absolutely sure.

My spirit knew something my heart did not—I had to return to my temporary home back on Earth. As I slid back into my physical body, I realized I was not at my home. I was on a gurney being wheeled into an emergency room. My pajamas were gone. I was wearing a hospital gown.

That thought bothered me far more than being on the other side. When had they taken my clothes off, who had taken them off me, and where were they now? Why was I here? Who are all these people staring down at me? I was confused and angry about being "back," and I felt like a prisoner confined in the density of my body.

Everything looked strange and different, as if I were trying to acclimate in an unfamiliar place. A nurse asked me if I could get into the bed by myself. I attempted to scoot off the gurney onto the bed. I still wasn't able to comprehend my surroundings. My body felt heavy, unable to move freely like it had before. I could not perform her request no matter how hard I tried. She held a pen in front of my face and asked me to identify it. I stared intently at this long object, and yet I had no recollection of what it was, or who she was, because I was still adjusting back into my body.

She called in a neurologist to evaluate my condition. Since I didn't have the ability to recognize a pen, he felt I should be admitted, and have an MRI to see if there was any damage to my brain. I was still trying to solve the mystery of why I was in the hospital in the first place.

To understand how I felt, consider being in a deep sleep. Someone wakes you in an abrupt manner. You are in an unfamiliar room and bright lights shine in your face. Strangers surround you. You are asked questions that you cannot answer; it's an interrogation. Do you feel confused and overwhelmed by the chaos? I sure did.

A couple of hours later, I was transported by ambulance to another hospital. The paramedics and I engaged in a lively conversation about quantum physics, and the existence of other realities beyond Earth. Because of the lunar eclipse, I begged them to take me outside and let me watch. They said no and apologized because it was after midnight and their shift was ending, but I appreciated the kindness they showed me.

The next day, the MRI scan results were in and the neurologist determined that I might have had a Transient Ischemic Attack (TIA), because there was a pinpoint dot at the top of my brain (my crown chakra). He'd also determined my potassium levels were dangerously depleted, and that might have contributed to the "shutdown."

***

A couple of weeks later, during an evaluation of my health by Dr. Mohammad, he asked me to recall my experience. He listened intently, and then assured me that he had heard about this kind of 'journey' before. He had jotted down notes of my 'journey' when I was admitted. My memory of that conversation with him was blurry. Journey? I called it a "stroke of luck" because I was able to experience life on the other side and see my dad again. What an amazing gift that I will cherish forever.

When I finally got up the nerve to discuss this experience with a few people I trusted, they all asked the same question: "If you were truly on the other side, why didn't Sean show up?"

This is a valid point. It wasn't that I didn't want to see my dad, but I was desperate to see Sean again. Why hadn't he met me on that "journey" to complete my "stroke of luck?"

***

Several months later, I was able to ask Susanne Wilson about the experience. She confirmed that I had been to the other side. I told her I believed I had, but needed validation, and couldn't figure out why Sean wasn't part of it.

What she said next allowed me to gain perfect clarity. "Linda," she said, "if you had been able to see Sean, you would have decided to stay. You were supposed to die that day, it was one of your exit points, but your time here is not up, and you still have a mission to complete."

Since my dad and I were very close, it made sense that he would show up to comfort me. That is what a parent would do, of course. He rushed to the aid of his child to alleviate any fear I might have had as I entered my new surroundings. I didn't imagine it, because Sean would have been the focal point; not my dad.

But where was I? Where did I go? I have no idea, except that it was another physical dimension, one of a higher frequency than Earth. I know that the experience was as real as this life. In fact, it's more so.

CHAPTER 12
Did I Agree?

Reality is merely an illusion, albeit a very persistent one.
~ Albert Einstein

The reality is that everyone is meant to die. There are no exceptions.

Some of the atheist NDE experiencers with whom I had spoken still didn't believe in God or a higher power. However, they did tell me that they are no longer afraid to die because they were still conscious of their state of being during their aborted exit point. Considering all the people with whom I have spoken on this topic, the consensus is that death is a beautiful process, and they felt free and happy. Perhaps how one gets there isn't so pleasant, but the actual experience of crossing over is pure joy.

Western culture shuns the discussion of death. It is a taboo word. When it happens, people are always shocked. Then there is a consensus as to whether the death was warranted…or not. In other words, if a person reaches a particular age, is considered elderly, then it is permissible to die. If someone is very sick, then after a designated amount of time, they are given permission to depart because they have suffered enough. When a young person dies, it is out-of-order, unacceptable, and should have never happened. Parents aren't supposed to outlive their children. Period. When it happened to me, I noticed that many of my peers disappeared from my life. Perhaps they feared what befell me would happen to them. Perhaps they just didn't know what to say, like so many of the people I met along the way, who avoid death at all costs.

I understand and respect their decisions, but I now have a different, broader perspective. It's a new way of looking at the energy of human life…in its totality.

Pierre Teilhard de Chardin wrote: "We are not human beings having a spiritual experience. We are spiritual beings having a human experience." But, as humans, we look at the chronological age of a person as a marker for life expectancy. This is normal—when your perspective is rooted in the timeline from birth to death. I challenge you to look at it in a different way, and ask yourself this: Could the concepts of linear time and linear consciousness be wrong? Could form encounter formless and provide the necessary elements to allow a person to expand their perspective of reality?

Based on all the research and information that I have collected I believe that each person makes agreements for the experience of a life on Earth with a soul group before birth. I believe in reincarnation. Earth is a great school to acquire knowledge, and people are able to learn a lot in its operating system. Why wouldn't a soul's energy transition in and out of different eras of linear time in order to experience unique sequences?

And, since it is always more valuable to learn in groups, soul energies can agree with other soul energies to create lives where they come into contact on Earth to give and take together. They may form a soul group to travel with through various lives, over and over, to advance spiritual growth and to learn. Such soul agreements are not intended to be set in stone. The idea of free will is very much at play as a force for creativity. As a group, each individual may incarnate again as a segment of their soul to advance spiritual growth and learn. They decide what lessons the group will learn, the roles they'll take on, and plan general themes for significant life events and lifestyles.

Why does this make sense to me?

One of my most challenging life lessons was the passing of my son. I questioned why children like Sean were never given an opportunity to live long productive lives, and experience all that life has to offer. It felt unfair to me, and I was angry with God for taking my child. Why couldn't he have taken me? I would gladly have exchanged my death for his life. However, when I asked these "Why?" questions to all who would listen, and even to the spirit energies I could not see but believed in, the explanation I received felt right: We are here to explore the many opportunities to live, and to die, and to learn, and to exist.

Think about this. Perhaps your agreement with the soul who chose to be your child in this lifetime was that he or she incarnated to teach you how to feel unconditional love and to show great compassion. I know that for myself, I didn't truly understand the meaning of love until I had a baby. I had never allowed my heart to open and receive love fully due to a fear of being abandoned. However, when I took a first look at my baby Shannon and my baby Sean, my heart opened completely—and stayed that way. The love I felt for them was indeed unconditional. I now know that unconditional love was one of the many lessons I came here to master. I say I know this, because for most of my life I kept my heart shielded, for fear of being hurt or rejected. My heart wore a coat of armor as protection from the outside world.

It wasn't until I had children that all these concealed emotions came rushing into my life. The responsibility of a parent, and the impact they have on their children's perception of life, is critical to their emotional and spiritual growth. I would do anything for my children, and surrounding them with love and safety was, and still is, my main purpose in life.

I didn't understand this as a child, but after my father died and I was told he was sleeping—only to discover that he was never coming home—my trust was broken. A sense of abandonment and also betrayal seeped into my consciousness, and I wasn't aware of this impact until I became an adult. I found myself questioning everything and everyone. Were they telling me the truth, or just telling me what they wanted me to believe? I was very cautious about where I invested myself. Many people thought I was shy or aloof, but I was learning about trust—in relationships, in school, at work, at play, and in religion. Unknowingly, I was assessing their energetic fields to determine whom I could trust.

***

Before I got married, I returned to Catholicism. It seemed like the logical thing to do at the time since my soon-to-be family was Catholic. We joined the local parish church and assumed all the duties and responsibilities of Catholicism. Shannon and Sean were baptized and attended Sunday school for years, while we attended Mass.

This practice changed around the time of Shannon's confirmation. When she was going through the pre-confirmation process, I was called into the rectory office. The priest was upset. He told me to get her in line or he wasn't going to confirm her.

I wondered why he thought she was she out-of-line. What was her sin?

It was because she questioned why she had to confess to him, and then he had to speak to God on her behalf. She asked why she could not just go to God directly.

I thought that was a fair and logical question, but the priest took great offense to it. He wasn't going to budge. Since confirmation was only a week away, I relented and talked with Shannon. I explained that if she just went along, there would be a big party afterwards, with gifts for her. Then, if she wanted to leave the church, she had my blessing. I had no reason to keep her there after that fiasco.

She agreed. After confirmation, she left the church.

Sean's confirmation was a year later. Same scenario. He left the church as Shannon had done.

I think religion has its place, but for us, the rigidity of the Church was something that no longer resonated in our lives. Looking back now at my entire life, I'm not sure if it ever did. I needed to step away. How could I ever make room for myself to expand in a space with such demanding limitations? I didn't expect our extended family to understand, but I hoped they would honor our choices, as we honored theirs.

Instilling fear into a child and threatening them with the ability to withhold a sacrament was the pivotal point. Living with angst was not how I wanted my children to experience the love of God. I'd lived in fear while attending church and didn't want that for them. I knew it was time for us to leave and find another way to connect with God on our own terms. I hoped that they would find something that resonated with their soul, and not just accept what had been passed down through generations which reverberated the vibrations of control and fear.

That logic no longer worked for us. We had to follow our hearts. Shannon studied Judaism, and Sean explored Buddhism. It made sense to them and I completely understood. I even attended a synagogue service with Shannon and enjoyed the rituals and beauty of Judaism's rich history.

While being the mother of a child who passed at a young age was a tough agreement for me, I believe we all seem to have agreed to share a lifetime with a spiritual curriculum.

CHAPTER 13
The Energy of Love

*I'm not afraid of death because I don't believe in it.
It's just getting out of one car, and into another.*
~ John Lennon

The energy of love is the only remainder of the physical life humans leave behind. How well was love given and received? What memories of love linger?

I believe that love is an energy that exists on both sides of the veil. Remember this: Buddha wasn't Buddhist, Jesus wasn't a Christian, and Muhammad wasn't a Muslim. For each of these leaders, 'religion' was 'love.' These spiritual masters taught about the power of love, and about the continuation of life after the physical death of the body.

Science and spirituality are more alike than different, but many scientists have difficulty admitting this to be true. Science shows how energy cannot be destroyed, how it changes form. Think of the water in an ice cube. It appears solid when frozen, however, when it melts to room temperature, it changes from solid into liquid. When this water is boiled, it transitions from liquid into vapor. It's still the same water, just in a different form. Spirituality also shows that humans take on a solid, physical form for life, but at death, the soul 'evaporates' out of the body.

As solid ice turns into water that turns into steam, human beings turn into energy into spirit. So, if the person-soul isn't extinguished by death, they can figure out ways to use their new energy to visit loved ones who are still in the physical world.

Energy doesn't lie. Energy tells its own truths.

Lights can turn on when no human hand flips the switch or starts the electrical current.

Glass can shatter due to a force unseen.

And spirits can hug humans.

***

One afternoon, a few months after Sean's spirit crossed over, I became very tired while doing work on the computer. I left the desk and sat on the couch. My eyelids felt heavy, as if had lead weights on them; I could not keep them open no matter how hard I tried. Then something incredible happened.

I felt Sean hugging me.

His arms encircled me from behind as they'd done many times when he was alive while giving me a surprise bear hug. I could feel the hairs on his arms, and the smell of his cologne. I lifted up his left hand and kissed it. Then I felt the warmth of his right arm as it brushed against my cheek. I kissed it. I told him how much I loved him.

A few seconds later, the hug was over, and he was gone. I opened my eyes.

No, I wasn't sleeping. I was however, in a light hypnagogic state—between wakefulness and sleep. I was also on a high because I had just received a hug from my son in spirit!

I knew no one was going to believe me, so I kept it to myself for a long time.

***

I later learned that spirits have an easier time communicating with humans as they move between full conscious awareness and a sleep state. I am forever bonded with the love for my son both in his physical form, and non-form. At that moment I realized that I was being shown how to navigate the delicate dance of duality between both worlds, entwining them in an intricate pattern to form the fundamental structure of reality. This journey has become my sacred passage, an experience I want to pass on to all who are open to receiving it.

A woman I met at the AREI conference told me about a similar encounter with the spirit of her son. She said, "I know you probably aren't going to believe me, but I need to share this with you for some reason. I didn't believe in the existence of an afterlife, but I missed my son so much that I was desperate to hear, see, and smell anything that resembled him. I was doing laundry, and when I came around the corner, my son was standing there. Not a vision where I could see just an outline, but he was physically there."

She said she thought she was losing her mind. He came over to her and gave her a hug. She could feel the shirt he wore and the warmth of his breath as he kissed the top of her head. He told her he was fine and not to worry. Then he gave her one last hug.

It was so sudden and unexpected that she didn't know what to think. She couldn't tell anyone in her family for fear that they would immediately negate her experience and suggest she be on medication. She was seeing a grief counselor and shared the encounter only to be told it was her imagination and best not to share it with others. This woman realized she needed a new counselor. She knew what she experienced was real.

So did I! I knew my hug experience wasn't wishful thinking. Even though I didn't see Sean, I'd felt that kind of hug from him many times in the past. It made perfect sense for him to continue in spirit as a way to let me know he was still near. I emailed an account of my hug from Sean to two of brilliant researchers I'd met at the AREI conference: Gary Schwartz, Ph.D., and Mark Pitstick, M.A., D.C. They each wrote back to assure me that the encounter was not just my imagination. I was elated and relieved.

***

Encounters with the feeling of a spirit's energy are common. Many people are much more open now about having seen and felt their loved ones who have crossed over. I've heard and read many stories about deceased spouses who come to reassure their partners with a touch; spirit siblings reaching out to still-living siblings through the use of familiar sounds in unexpected ways; grandparents who have been an integral part of their families reappearing; and, deceased friends generating the scent of their signature perfume in an attention-getting way to another friend.

Remember—spirits use whatever energetic means necessary to show those still on Earth that they are fine, especially the first year after their transition back to their home. Our senses have been dulled by the atrophy of limited beliefs, and our loved ones work incredibly hard to help us to remember that separation is only an illusion. Separation is the core myth of death, and unfortunately, it is the core myth of our American culture.

For many years, I wondered if I was being led down a path of illusions while searching for an imagined state of consciousness called happiness. The moments of happiness I experienced were temporary when I allowed society's norms to dictate my version of happiness. I think this is true for the people who feel as if they are just existing, the people whose dreams were shattered by fear, turmoil, chaos, violence, disappointments, betrayal, anger, and hatred. Humans seem to be born with basic innate fears, and as they age, the fears expand beyond the person's capacity to navigate them. Human souls become exhausted, emotionally, physically, and spiritually. I choose to believe that each of us will decide how we will navigate the chaos, as part of our decision to experience a physical life. Do we dare cross the bridge and close the gap between the physical and non-physical worlds that exist beyond our limited senses?

Everyone has more than enough fears—there is no need to add fear of death to the list. People are born to die, it's that simple and yet so complicated for many to comprehend.

My own inner chaos was fear of the unknown, and it was my greatest obstacle to growth. I knew that in order to direct my life in a way that made sense for me, I had to discover how to alleviate my fears, and that was through knowledge and understanding. The more I connected with the ability to perceive a consciousness beyond my limited physical senses, the more my fear dissipated. This is of course my own journey and story. Each person must navigate their own life accordingly. I worked to transform my 'unknown' into a knowing that consciousness is a never-ending flow of intelligence, available to anyone willing to reach out and touch it. As I did, the myth of death and dying was washed away from my energetic field.

***

After Sean's transition, I thought I would never find joy in my life again. I continually pursued it, only to find it slipping away as soon as I got near. Then one day I came to the realization that when I stopped searching, joy found me.

I was dancing and having fun again.

With the birth of my grandson Thomas Patrick (Shannon and Eddie's son), new life energy and love entered my world. The circle of life continues on. I know on a soul level, Sean and Tommy know each other well.

I've chosen to shape my reality through the power of love.

Love is the imprint people leave on the hearts of others before transitioning back to their rightful place in the spiritual realm. In reality, humans own nothing—they are just custodians of Earth life. Love, however, is something that will remain forever.

My desire is to change the way humanity views death. It is not the end, but the continuation of the life known while in the body, transferred to a pure energetic form after physical death. The sacred dance between life and death is one that we will all be called on to perform. My hope is that after reading this book you will not run from the dance but embrace it as your partner with love and gratitude for the experience and reverence for this life you were given to live.

So, on a final note, here's the English nursery rhyme that originated in 1852 that, to me, describes life in a perfect way:

Row, row, row your boat
gently down the stream.
Merrily, merrily, merrily, merrily,
life is but a dream.

CONCLUSION

Outside of our blood family, there are soul family members. These are people that I truly believe are guided into our lives at a specific time for a reason. Who or what guided them? I am not certain. Perhaps it was a pre-birth agreement. The 'whys' are not important. The fact that they are here is important to me.

I have a number of soul family members who've come and gone in my life, each who brought a gift along the way that I will always cherish. Some have entered for a short period of time; others stayed for decades, and with others, our relationships continue to evolve.

***

One person who has been in my life for decades and will continue to be until I transition home (and likely afterwards, too) is my best friend, Ann. I met her when we were teens and just beginning to discover the mysteries of life. We have a bond that is closer than many blood relatives and we have supported each other through some of the happiest and also the most heartbreaking times of our life. Weeks and even months will go by without us speaking, and yet without a doubt, we will pick up right where we left off, never missing a beat.

As I mentioned, Ann was the first person to meet me in Virginia Beach. She stayed by my side as long as I needed her, and I could see the pain in her eyes that she felt for me. Feeling helpless, and yet wanting desperately to do something to make the situation tolerable, is the best explanation of what I saw in her—reflecting back to me. I am so grateful she was there. Her Southern accent, as well as her quirky euphemisms, keep me laughing and that is one of the greatest gifts she has given me. I know that no matter what happens, or how much time passes, the connection we share is always with us.

***

Paula is another soul family member. I met her in 2016 after I won a gift that she'd donated when we were at a conference. Later, I called to inquire about the details, and she mentioned that she'd attempted to meet me after a lecture Susanne Wilson gave at a local bookstore. Paula said she had been sitting in the row behind me as I received messages from Sean that Susanne delivered. However, I left before we had a chance to connect. We agreed to meet for lunch, and there was an immediate connection between us. Hours passed as we conversed about a myriad of subjects, including the afterlife. Her ability to ascertain and grasp the teachings was impressive, especially coming from a clinical background in the field of counseling. She and I shared our experiences and even attended the AREI conference in Scottsdale together to further our education.

What I soon realized, was that Paula is endowed with an ability as a spirit artist. She connects with other realms, receives messages and paints or draws those who are in spirit. She gifted me with paintings of my guides; I have them displayed in my home office. They are a beautiful reminder that I am always in their presence.

Paula has been an invaluable friend to me, especially since I felt so lost at times after Sean's passing. Her words are always reassuring, and occasionally she delivers funny messages from him at the perfect time. This keeps my heart light and happy. I believe that she and I have had other lifetimes together. That was something we both felt soon after we met, perhaps as a reminder of our life's mission.

***

My sister-in-law Kathy completes the triad of my soul family members. I have known her for over 30 years, but it wasn't until Sean passed, that something wonderful shifted in our relationship. She was there every step of the way, offering a shoulder to cry on when often that was the only thing I was capable of doing.

Kathy shared with me her mystical encounters with Sean and expressed how incredible it was that they were happening to her. We talked for hours, reminiscing about the silly antics Shannon and Sean would pull on other members of the family. These moments of joy helped to heal parts of my heart that were shattered.

We have helped each other through some very difficult times in our lives. There is a bond between us that will last always. When we rented a house in California for Shannon's wedding, Joyce and her family had the opportunity to spend quality time with Kathy. There was no awkwardness, just lots of laughter and fun. I am grateful that Kathy is a part of my soul family.

ABOUT THE AUTHOR

Linda M. McCarthy, Ph.D., holds a doctorate as a board-certified Metaphysical Counselor, with a certification in Spirituality and Grieving. She is an ordained minister, a Usui reiki master, an afterlife researcher, and an educator. Linda's purpose is to share her experience as a parent with a child in spirit and to provide resources to help those with loved ones on the other side to heal. Having researched the work of brilliant minds in the fields of medicine, law, and science, as well as her own personal experience on the other side, Linda says, "I know, without a shadow of a doubt, that we survive physical death, we thrive afterwards, and we will definitely see our loved ones again."

RESOURCE MATERIALS

This section of the book is not a typical research database of information. It is meant to be shared with attorneys, researchers, doctors, scientists, engineers, health care workers, teachers, and even evidential mediums—anyone who is searching for the same answer to one of life's biggest questions: Is there life after death?

There were many books I read for research; some were written by open-minded skeptics, some authors were atheists, others were non-believers of evidence of any reality that comes after physical life. I read with an unbiased perspective. Some of these books were like stepstools; others were ladders as they allowed me to climb higher on my path of discovery about what happens after the transition from physicality. I am grateful to the medical doctors for their willingness to share their patients' experiences, as well as their own, on the other side of the veil.

I did my own research with evidential mediums by receiving a reading from or taking a class taught by them. In one case, I was given a complimentary reading. These beautiful souls came into my life at different times in the years since Sean's transition. They have impressed me with their ability to communicate with Sean, and they've verified for me information I've received from him through my own innate ability. These individuals are gifted people with a capacity to heal the broken hearts of those left behind after the death of a loved one.

From this point forward, you will find information about the individuals who've shared their experiences and their expertise with me; some are authors whose books informed my own writing.

EBEN ALEXANDER, M.D.

Dr. Alexander graduated from Duke University School of Medicine and completed his Neurosurgery residency at Duke University Medical Center in 1987. He continued his education with a Cerebrovascular Neurosurgery fellowship at Newcastle General Hospital in the United Kingdom the following year. With over 25 years of neurosurgical training, Dr. Alexander experienced a multitude of brain trauma cases including aneurysms, infections, tumors, and strokes.

His extensive training was completely altered when he has had his own experience on the other side due to a severe case of acute bacterial meningoencephalitis in his brain. He was given less than a 10 percent chance of survival. None of his peers believed he would fully recover. While in a deep coma, Dr. Alexander met a deceased sister—who had been unknown to him since he was adopted. He traveled through beautiful dimensions and had incredible journeys with her that he describes in his book, *Proof of Heaven*.

That book gave me joy in knowing that we didn't have to physically die in order to have these experiences. I know for myself I didn't have the vernacular to describe what I had gone through. After reading his book and speaking with Dr. Alexander, I felt more comfortable to discuss my own journey with ease and love, rather than fear of condemnation. His books have brought understanding and hope to the hearts of many readers.

You can find out more about his incredible journey both as a physician, and on the other side at **http://ebenalexander.com**.

MARK ANTHONY

Mark Anthony is known as The Psychic Lawyer. His gift of communication with the afterlife spans four generations. An evidential medium, Mark was educated at Oxford and is licensed to practice law in Florida and Washington, D.C. His ability to discern fact from fiction is one of the reasons he is so well respected in both law and mediumship.

I had the good fortune to hear Mark speak at a conference and know that he brings spirit messages through with accuracy and brings comfort to those who are in his presence.

You can find more information about Mark's work and his bestselling book, *Evidence of Eternity*, on his website: **www.evidenceofeternity.com**.

KAT BAILLIE

Kat Baillie is a talented British evidential medium, clairvoyant, and intuitive. She was trained by some of the United Kingdom's leading mediums as well as healers. Before becoming a full time medium, Kat was the head buyer for the British fashion industry.

I was introduced to Kat through Helping Parents Heal. She had been rigorously tested before being accepted into that organization. She is a beacon of light and her smile is genuine and warm. Kat wasted no time in bringing me evidence that she was speaking to Sean.

At one point during the reading, I thought to myself, "I would just like to have a fun conversation with Sean for a little while."

A moment later, Kat said, "Sean mentioned that you wanted to chat for a little while so let's do it." Through Kat, Sean talked about my new haircut, our dog Banshee, and the book I was beginning to write. He talked about the shorts he used to wear in 2014 that were shorter than normal. Kat saw he was wearing a pair and showing off his legs. As she described what she was envisioning, we both began laughing at his dry sense of humor. I kept that pair of Sean's shorts in a drawer at home.

Kat is incredibly accurate and communicates with spirit in a unique manner. I remember thinking she was magical the way she connected with the other side. She works with clients by computer or phone. Either way, her readings are spot-on. She works with Helping Parents Heal UK.

If you would like to contact Kat, or find out more information, her website is: **https://www.kat-b.com**.

STEFFANY BARTON

Steffany Barton is a psychic medium and author who specializes in "angel readings." She provides public demonstrations and gives the spiritual community a voice. Steffany is a registered nurse, and is certified in past life regression, as well as hypnotherapy. She offers classes in spiritual development and is the author of three books.

I first learned about Steffany in 2015 from a friend who experienced a reading with her. I purchased an email reading from her where I could ask up to five questions. She didn't want any information ahead of time. Her response came back to me within a couple of days with answers that were on point. I sensed great integrity in her character and passion for the work she does.

Approximately six months later I had a phone reading with her, and she exceeded my expectations. Her sweet voice, and laughter, along with precise validations, left me with a sense of comfort and peace. She confirmed what I'd heard from other mediums and added more important pieces to the puzzle I wanted to solve.

If you would like to have a reading with Steffany, here is her contact information: **https://www.angelsinsight.com/**.

MICHELLE BELTRAN

Michelle began her career in the Air Force, specializing in law enforcement, and she traveled throughout the world. She implemented one of the first K-9 Narcotics Divisions in California, and loved working with her canine partner, Kilo. She was a professional cyclist and received two invitations to the Olympic Training Center in Colorado Springs. Michelle's intuitive ability as well as her gift for mediumship comes naturally. A second-generation psychic, she obtained formal training through the Mystic Shift Mediumship Program.

I honestly feel I was led by spirit to Michelle. I was looking for a medium with great credibility as well as a background in law enforcement. I contacted her only a few weeks after Sean transitioned. I was emotionally raw, and I know Michelle felt it. Her validations over the span of 30 minutes were very accurate. In addition, she shared unknown information with me that I had to confirm with family members. It all was factual. This was my first experience with an evidential medium, and I am so fortunate that it was with Michelle. She spoke with authority, just as I would expect from someone who had been in law enforcement. She also had gentleness in her voice, and much compassion. After our call, I felt for the first time in weeks a few moments of peace in my sea of grief.

There is a good reason Michelle has a large following. She is remarkably accurate and encompasses many other aspects of guidance in her work that is not just mediumship. Michelle can be found here: **https://michellebeltran.com/**.

STAFFORD BETTY, PH.D.

Stafford Betty Ph.D. is a professor of religious studies at California State University Bakersfield. He earned a doctorate in Asian religion at Fordham University. He authored many books on the afterlife. When I read *The Afterlife Unveiled*, one of the first things that struck me was the description of heaven by the spirits on the other side. They didn't refer to it as heaven, but as a multitude of realms beginning at the Earth's surface and extending outwards. I had never heard the heavenly realms described in that manner, and it brought me peace, knowing that we are all part of these realms, even in the physical body. This book delivered such comfort and confirmed my 'knowing' that deceased loved ones truly are right here with me, and all of us. Our realms merge, just in different dimensional frequencies. This book also granted me permission to speak aloud to my loved ones in spirit without fear of condemnation.

Dr. Betty's work is featured on this site: **https://www.csub.edu/~sbetty/welcome.html**.

ELIZABETH BOISSON

Elizabeth Boisson is the president and co-founder of the non-profit organization Helping Parents Heal (HPH). This organization assists bereaved parents with a multitude of resources, including online meetings, private pages on social media, and by organizing meetings all over the country and world for parents grieving the loss of children. The difference in this organization is that every parent is allowed to speak freely about their experience without judgment. Having an open dialogue about the afterlife is encouraged, and everyone, regardless of their beliefs, is allowed membership.

After two of Elizabeth's children transitioned to the other side (Chelsey in 1991 and Morgan in 2009), she joined forces with Mark Ireland in 2012 to create Helping Parents Heal. A yoga instructor, Elizabeth offers classes to help with the grieving process, as well as physical well-being.

I heard Elizabeth speak at a conference about the afterlife in Scottsdale, and then had the opportunity to meet her. I joined Helping Parents Heal shortly thereafter. Elizabeth is compassionate and caring—a shining example of what every parent hopes to be. She represents parents who know their child is very much alive and thriving on the other side. Elizabeth introduced me to an amazing group of parents who were there to assist me in any way they could. She also suggested some talented evidential mediums. After a couple of years as a member, I became a Caring Listener with this organization.

In 2018, HPH had their first conference for parents with children in spirit. It was filled to capacity with parents, speakers from all over the world, and break-out classes specializing in certain healing and communications modalities. I remember looking around and thinking, what a brave group of souls to be here and share their stories with the strangers who would instantly become part of their 'HPH family.' Elizabeth is a catalyst for bringing these connections to fruition and making a difference in the lives of thousands of parents and family members. There are now HPH individual groups for siblings as well as for fathers only. HPH members truly are a family, and Elizabeth is an angel here on Earth.

The website for HPH is: **www.helpingparentsheal.org**.

MICHELLE CLAIRE

Michelle Claire is a gifted intuitive coach and evidential medium. She has had a natural ability to contact with spirit all of her life—at first with her deceased grandparents. After experiencing multiple NDEs, including head trauma in 2011, Michelle's connection with spirit grew exponentially. She realized that her mission was to come back and help others to reconnect with their loved ones.

I was first introduced to Michelle's incredible ability during a Helping Parents Heal meeting in Phoenix. She began bringing in the children of the parents attending the meeting, and it happened so quickly that at one point, while she was reading for three parents, she asked their children to stand in line so she could be as accurate as possible. During her readings, she had the group laughing; many parents were shedding tears of joy with a knowing that their child was right there with them in the room. Her validations were remarkable, and I could see the shift in the parent's energy after the meeting was over.

Michelle offered to read for me, and I was astonished with her ability to connect so quickly and accurately with my loved ones in spirit. She reiterated some of the previous validations I had received from other mediums, however Michelle also shared vital information and answers to questions that until then, were elusive to me.

You can find out more information about Michelle at: **https://www.michelleclare.net**.

CAROLYN CLAPPER

A friend of mine who lives in Los Angeles, Bob, introduced me to Carolyn. He spoke highly of Carolyn's ability to connect with spirit as well as her gift to help others with health issues.

Carolyn explained that she was skeptical of modalities like mediumship. Although she described herself as "spiritual," she noted that connections with the spiritual realm did not resonate with her...until she had a severe case of meningitis. She found herself on the other side of the veil and vowed that if she were returned to raise her son, she would dedicate her life to this work.

During my reading with Carolyn, one of the first things that impressed me was her integrity. She wasn't watching the clock; she was working with spirit, and for me, to bring peace and resolution. This reading took place approximately three years after Sean's transition, and I had more questions than answers at that point. Carolyn was like a detective, digging deeper, and connecting with those on her team who could help. I truly felt like I had a partner working with me to assist with the issues at hand.

When I asked, Carolyn told me about some potential health issues of family members. A few months later, I realized that she was accurate about my relatives' diagnoses and the time frame of events surrounding them.

Her contact information is on her website: **http://thenextworldmedium.com/**.

LARRY DOSSEY, M.D.

Larry Dossey is the former chief of staff of Medical City Dallas Hospital. He earned his degree from Southwestern Medical School, is an internationally known speaker at medical schools, and is a decorated battalion surgeon, having served in Vietnam. Dr. Dossey is the former co-chairman of the Panel on Mind/Body Interventions, National Center for Complementary and Alternative Medicine, National Institutes of Health. He is the executive editor of the peer-reviewed journal *EXPLORE: The Journal of Science and Healing*.

I first listened to Dr. Dossey in a radio interview as he discussed the survival of consciousness outside the brain, particularly NDEs, shortly after Sean transitioned: (**https://www.drmiller.com/larry-dossey/**). He believes consciousness survives at a very high level during an NDE. His summation of people meeting loved ones on the other side resonated with me because of my experience meeting my deceased dad who passed over 50 years ago. Dr. Dossey believes that these visions are not hallucinations—they are real phenomena.

In his book, *One Mind: How Our Individual Mind is Part of a Greater Consciousness and Why It Matters*, he examines how a person after having an NDE, came back to have skills that they did not possess before the experience. This kind of information is not taught in medical schools. I truly respect his perspective, because it resonates with my philosophy about the reality of death: the me that I am never dies. There is a unity of all that is and there is a transformation of views on death after an NDE. The evaporation of fear is the greatest gift that one can receive from his work.

I believe that Dr. Dossey is a visionary and a pioneer in this field. I did have the privilege of speaking with him on the telephone for a short period of time in early 2015, and his kindness and words of encouragement I will always remember.

Dr. Dossey's work is featured here: **http://www.dosseydossey.com/larry/default.html**.

DIANE EILEEN

A family member told me about Diane and how powerful and accurate her readings were. I knew I needed to meet her. This particular family member didn't believe in mediums, but when she saw the remarkable change in one of her friends who'd had a reading with Diane, she decided to share the experience with me.

I contacted Diane, and she was more than happy to schedule a reading. Her approach and delivery were very different than other readings, in that she spoke directly to Sean with a voice that was slightly altered from her own. I was only a few months into the grieving process, and Diane was able to bring Sean's personality thorough, loud and clear. At one point, she asked him the same question twice, and I will always remember his response.

He said in a frustrated tone, "Listen lady, I don't know how many times I have to tell you, the answer is still NO!" Sean was never disrespectful unless he was pushed beyond his patience level.

Diane said, "Sean is very strong, even though he has only been on the other side a few months." She also came through with validations personal to me, such as the nickname Sean called me. There is only one other medium who was able to validate our nicknames for each other.

I had a number of readings with Diane on and off throughout the years and consider her a dear friend. She will send me a solution to an issue I am having with pinpoint accuracy from Sean, even when I don't ask her. Diane's deep Buddhist devotion resonates with Sean; he too gravitated towards Buddhism. Their connection is one of trust and respect.

Diane is recommended here with my deepest gratitude.

STUART HAMEROFF, M.D.

Dr. Hameroff is an esteemed anesthesiologist and professor at the University of Arizona. He has studied consciousness from a quantum energy perspective. His writing catapulted me into a different stratosphere because he believes consciousness may arise from a quantum state in protein polymers called microtubules in the cells of the brain. The origin of consciousness (not one neurosurgeon can locate it) has always been a great mystery.

Personally, I always wondered where consciousness resided in the body, pondering questions like, "When we are under anesthesia, we lose consciousness, but where does it go?" Perhaps, at death, consciousness leaves its residence in the brain's microtubules and ventures into some quantum energy field outside the physical body. If a dying person is resuscitated, their conscious energy returns 'home,' to the microtubules.

In Dr. Hameroff's first book *Ultimate Computing: Biomolecular Consciousness and NanoTechnology*, he introduced the public to the role of microtubules, and consciousness. This book discusses how the brain process information, and it is the foundation for the work he continues today—to find the location of consciousness in the human body. I continually follow his work, and publications for peer review, and am thrilled to see some of his fellow physicians opening up to the possibility that there may be more to consciousness than is taught in medical school.

If you would like more information on Dr. Hameroff's work, you can find it here: **http://www.quantumconsciousness.org/**.

R. CRAIG HOGAN, PH.D.

Dr. Hogan is the director of the Center for Spiritual Understanding, an organization that helps people maintain a relationship with loved ones on the other side. He has co-authored a number of books related to afterlife communication and is the author of one of my favorite books: *Your Eternal Self*. He serves on a number of boards, including the Academy of Spiritual and Paranormal Studies, the Association for Evaluation and Communication of Evidence for Survival, and the American Society for Standards in Mediumship and Psychical Investigation. He has been a professor of business communications and curriculum and is a training administrator at two universities and a medical school, as well as director of his own online business writing school.

When I was first introduced to Dr. Hogan, I found him to be both brilliant and one of the kindest people I'd ever had the privilege to meet. His database of knowledge was like an encyclopedia of the afterlife, but he spoke in terms anyone could understand. When I first read *Your Eternal Self*, I cried tears of joy to see that my knowing the afterlife is a reality and there is a continuation of life after the death of the physical body was confirmed.

Dr. Hogan has a free program for anyone interested in learning how to contact deceased loved ones. I have used it successfully and highly recommend it to anyone interested in afterlife communication. Here is the link to the site: **http://afterlifeconnections.org/craig.htm**.

THOMAS JOHN

Thomas John attended the University of Chicago where he earned, with honors, degrees in psychology and human development. He became the lead researcher at several prestigious universities, including a research internship at Yale, where he studied the relationship between psychopathology and personality. After being accepted into graduate programs in medical research, Thomas decided, due to direction from his team of loved ones on the other side, to continue to enhance his natural-born abilities as an intuitive and evidential medium in New York. Now Thomas is known as the Manhattan Medium, has his own television show spotlighting his abilities, is an author, and has an incredible fan base of celebrities.

I met Thomas through the classes that he offers online. At the end of each class, he selects a few students and gives a quick reading for them. I was fortunate to receive one. Thomas brought Sean in and mentioned that I slept with his pillows. True. He also validated that I had two tattoos. True. Before I could ask, he accurately answered my written questions.

After waiting a year, I contacted him for a full reading. One message from that reading stands out in my mind. Thomas asked me if I was going to buy a piece of property and I told him no.

He said, "Spirit says you are, so just write that down."

I wrote it down but had no intention of purchasing any property. I know that mediums are never 100 percent accurate, but Thomas was in the high 90s for accuracy on other issues with me.

Fast forward four months. I purchased a timeshare at a beach. I had completely forgotten about the message Thomas had given me. Then one evening as I was going through my notes, there it was!

Thomas offers a myriad of services on his website: **www.mediumthomas.com**.

ISABELLA JOHNSON

Healing physically, emotionally, and spiritually is the trifecta that Isabella Johnson offers in a unique and personal way. She is a certified evidential medium, a grief recovery specialist, medical intuitive, and a remote viewer. As a mother with a child in spirit, Isabella understands how vitally important it is to make a connection with them.

Another gift Isabella offers her clients is to intuitively see medical issues in the body and release the symptoms of disease. She is able to see the soul's energy and enable a person to be empowered by knowing their life's purpose.

I was introduced to Isabella through Helping Parents Heal. The first reading I received was a 30-minute telephone session, and the messages came through with rapid fire. It was all I could do to keep up with her.

Later, I attended a meeting at Helping Parents Heal and Isabella was the speaker. Even though she is petite in stature, her energetic presence is large. The first thing that made me smile was that she asked if she could take off her shoes. Of course, no one objected, and after a few minutes of sharing her story with all of us, the readings ensued. Validation after validation continued for over an hour. I was astonished at her accuracy and compassion as well as empathy for all the parents in the room. She shared with all of us that she would bring through what we needed to hear, not necessarily what we wanted to hear. The amount of healing she delivered to parents that day was remarkable.

Months later, I scheduled a Facebook video session with her. The appointment was for an hour. I had a notepad, but also knew to record it, because the messages and information would flow so quickly. Isabella brought in Sean; she also brought through my mom and dad. They were there just to substantiate their presence with Sean. She delivered information that I had not heard before and told me about the personalities of family members who happened to be non-believers or highly skeptical, which was accurate. Isabella was able to connect with a family member who has dementia and relay messages to me that this person is unable to give otherwise.

It was heartwarming, incredibly detailed, and specific. Isabella mentioned that at some point in the next year, my family members would be more receptive to a reading. I have to be honest and say that I felt that the chances were slim.

Fast forward to 2019 when I purchased a reading for my daughter, the open-minded skeptic. Isabella was able to reconnect Shannon with Sean and enable a wonderful conversation. Shannon told me that she was absolutely sure she was talking to her brother!

Eventually, Kevin decided to have a reading with Isabella—likely to confirm his belief that mediums are vague and don't provide any credible evidence. Isabella changed his mind. He was blown away with her validations. There were confirmations, and personal messages that only he would understand. But there was one validation he was looking for and didn't receive. When he asked her about it, she said, "Don't tell me what it is, and when I get a chance, I will connect with your son and ask."

Several days later, she called him back and he received the evidence he needed. He went from being a closed-minded skeptic to a believer. In fact, so much so, that he actually wrote a review on her website. Isabella changed the dynamics of my family and I am grateful.

If you would like more information about Isabella, here is her website: https://thesoulreadingmedium.com/.

DEBRA MARTIN

Debra Martin is naturally gifted, but her abilities heightened after a multitude of "shifts," as she calls them. She had two horrific car accidents in which she should not have survived. One was in 1997, the other 2000. In both incidences, she believed that divine intervention saved her life. She heard a voice ask her "Are you ready?" after the second accident. When she responded that no, she wasn't ready, she was thrust back into her body and the vehicle. At that point, she realized she had been somewhere else, not in this Earth realm. She also suffered a terrible illness that almost took her life in 2011. After recovering, her abilities became even stronger.

A Windbridge certified research medium, Debra is also a lab certified medium with the Forever Family Foundation. Dr. Gary Schwartz tested her at his facility in Tucson, under rigorously controlled conditions. She is a gifted medium, and also has an ability to heal others, remotely or in person. She wrote about her experiences and healings in her latest book, *Proof of Miracles*. She consulted in police investigations for missing persons and even homicide cases. Debra is also an ordained minister.

I met Debra through Helping Parents Heal when she offered a demonstration for a group in Phoenix. Her ability to bring spirit through with accuracy, as well as share her experiences with healing others who were close to death, was impressive. Debra's connection with my loved ones was exceptional at that meeting. She shared situations that had recently occurred to validate that my loved ones on the other side knew exactly what was happening in my life. She also responded with answers to questions I had not yet asked aloud.

For more information on Debra and the services she offers, her website is: https://www.goldenmiracles.com/. Here is information on the studies being conducted at Windbridge Institute: **http://www.windbridge.org/** and the Forever Family Foundation: **https://www.foreverfamilyfoundation.org/**.

LYNNE MCTAGGART

Lynne McTaggart is an award-winning journalist and has written a number of worldwide bestselling books. My favorite is *The Field*. She is known for her work with the field of consciousness and for consistently diving deep into research for answers to the questions about it. As an expert in the field of intention, she has shown how thoughts create powerful manifestations.

What resonated with me about the research that Lynn conducts, is that her beliefs shatter the paradigms of many other theories. She postulates that body and mind are not separate from the environment—they are constantly interacting with a field of energy that is alive and vibrant. She intertwines quantum physics with classic scientific work that has given me a much better understanding of how we interact with this invisible field of energy both in the physical and non-physical.

Lynne's work can be found here: **https://lynnemctaggart.com/**.

RAYMOND MOODY, M.D.

Dr. Raymond Moody is a physician, psychologist, and philosopher, as well as a bestselling author of many books on the afterlife and paranormal. He has been documenting the accounts of those who have had a physical death and then returned to describe their experience on the other side. Although each one was different, they all had similarities of feeling loved beyond words, with a conscious awareness that they were home. Dr. Moody's book, *Life After Life*, was one I'd read long ago. It discusses the possibility of the existence of spirit after death. This was in complete opposition of what I had been taught as a child. His wisdom brought me a sense of peace and released the fear that I was so accustomed to feeling through the lens of religion.

There has been criticism regarding Dr. Moody's work—namely that all the Near Death Experiences (NDEs) he described were different. However, I wonder how death is any different from people being dropped off at an amusement park and heading off in different directions from one another. There would be some commonalities, but also some very different experiences—so much so that observers might wonder if they were even in the same park. People who have had an NDE have a common denominator, but also each spirit is having their own experience in different realms or at different frequencies. My own NDE experience was unique to me, and I am sure that is the case for each person. Dr. Moody's book was the catalyst for me to dive deeper into the subject of the survival of consciousness, and I am thankful for his lifelong dedication to this work that he continues to this day.

DAISY MAE MOORE

Daisy Mae Moore is another British evidential medium who has had her abilities tested by Helping Parents Heal. She brings through indisputable evidence and is also a remote viewer. As a professional nurse working in palliative care, Daisy has been in the presence of patients who've crossed over and has been working with the spiritual realm for over 10 years. Also the parent of a child now in spirit, she understands the challenges parents face in grief.

I have had a number of readings with Daisy, and after she validates the presence of a loved one in spirit, she begins the conversation. She has offered remote viewing of my home to confirm certain items that have significant meaning to Sean. When she spoke of the details in a shadow box she saw that hangs on the wall in Kevin's office, I was astonished. She described a location in our backyard, next to a vegetable garden and wind chime—it is a place Sean's spirit comes to be with me when I sit there. Again, how could she know this? Her ability to perform remote viewing is a wonderful gift she willingly shares with others.

Daisy can be reached either by Facebook video, Skype, or Facetime through https://www.facebook.com/Daisymaemoore.medium.

MARY NEAL, M.D.

Mary Neal, M.D. graduated from the University of Kentucky, and completed her orthopedic surgery training at the University of Southern California (USC). She studied abroad for a year and a half, training in the specialty of spinal surgery, then returned to California to become the director of spine surgery at USC.

As a physician, her beliefs were pragmatic. She had questioned the existence of a God, or anything after death. It was in South America where she drowned while kayaking in 1999. She described that experience in a book, *To Heaven and Back*. Underwater for approximately 30 minutes, she vividly remembers being in the presence of a higher being—Jesus—and feeling surrounded by love. The intensity of her experience has not faded over time.

Her perspective on life before and life after her experience of being "kicked out of heaven," is one that I understand. The semantics may be different, but the experience of going from a possible belief to a knowing, is a commonality both we share.

Dr. Neal lectures all over the world, telling her remarkable story of survival. Her work continues to help others to understand that there is a continuation of life after physical death.

You can find more information about Dr. Neal on her website: http://drmarynealbooks.com/.

BOB OLSON

Bob Olson is strongly dedicated to debunking anyone who isn't able to present credible evidence without any shadow of a doubt. With a degree in criminology, he's worked as a private investigator specializing in fraud, personal injury, and homicide. As one who wasn't convinced that there was an afterlife, or even a higher source, Bob preferred evidence over belief. After the transition of his dad in 1997, Bob wanted to know if he'd survived death, or if he was just gone. This became the impetus for his investigative work and best-selling book, *Answers about the Afterlife*.

Now an afterlife investigator and researcher who works with psychics and mediums, Bob has rigorously tested hundreds of mediums to discern those who are legitimate from those who are not. His work and commitment to obtain factual data supporting his findings, enabled me to better understand that this work was being taken seriously by those who needed proof—not just hearsay.

You can read more about Bob Olson's work at: **www.afterlifetv.com**.

MARK PITSTICK, M.A., D.C.

Mark Pitstick has over 40 years of experience in counseling across many different environments: in churches, private practice, and work in mental health facilities. He also earned a doctorate in chiropractic health care and has a passion for teaching.

I met Dr. Pitstick at the 2015 AREI conference in Scottsdale, and he truly changed my life for the better. He was one of the first people I reached out to for assistance in my time of grief, even before I met him in person. The information he provided allowed me to navigate an unknown path with dignity and understanding. I read all the articles he wrote and posted on his website. I watched the videos of his lectures and read every book that he recommended. I can pick up the phone and call, or email Dr. Pitstick, and he will respond whenever he has a moment in his busy schedule. I am forever grateful for his kindness and friendship.

You can find more information about Dr. Pitstick on his website: **www.soulproof.com**.

MAX PLANCK, PH.D., FOSMEMRS

Max Planck (1858-1947), a Nobel Prize winner, is best known for his work in the field of theoretical physics and is considered the father of quantum physics. He wrote: "I regard consciousness as fundamental, I regard matter as a derivative of consciousness. We cannot get behind consciousness. Everything that we talk about, everything that regard as existing, postulates consciousness."

His work in quantum physics resonates with me with regard to the survival of consciousness. There is a hypothesis that the mind is independent of the outside world; it exists in a field of possibilities. Max Planck allows readers of his many books to gain insight into his immense contribution to the world of quantum physics, and a different perspective on physics in general. The Max Planck Society for the Advancement of Science has much more information on his incredible life-long body of work.

For more information, go to **https://www.britannica.com/topic/Max-Planck-Society-for-the-Advancement-of-Science**.

GARY SCHWARTZ, PH.D.

Dr. Gary Schwartz is a professor of psychology, medicine, neurology, psychiatry, and surgery. He is the Director of the Laboratory for Advances in Consciousness and Health (LACH), formerly the Human Energy Systems Laboratory at the University of Arizona. After receiving his doctorate from Harvard University, he served as a professor of psychology and psychiatry at Yale University, director of the Yale Psychophysiology Center, and co-director of the Yale Behavioral Medicine Clinic. Dr. Schwartz has published over 400 academic papers, edited 11 academic books, and is the author of several books including: *The Afterlife Experiments*; *The Truth about Medium: Extraordinary Experiments with the Real Allison DuBois of NBC's "Medium" and Other Remarkable Psychics*; *The G.O.D. Experiments*; and, *The Energy Healing Experiments*.

I met Dr. Schwartz in 2015 at the AREI conference in Scottsdale. Here was a scientist whose reputation was on the line, yet he spoke with such conviction that I found myself captivated by his extensive research. I had the opportunity to chat with him for a few minutes, and although he was quite busy, he took the time to answer my questions with compassion and kindness.

You can find more information about Dr. Schwartz at **https://lach.arizona.edu/**.

K. PAUL STROLLER, M.D.

Dr. Stroller completed his pediatric training at the University of California Los Angeles School of Medicine in 1986. As a board-certified pediatrician, his expertise is in brain injury, and he practiced in the field of functional medicine, also known as integrative medicine. Dr. Stroller was also an adjunct assistant professor at A.T. Still University School of Osteopathic Medicine in Arizona.

What I respect about Dr. Stoller, as a physician/scientist, is that after the transition of his son Galen in 2007 due to an accident, he began actively searching for answers as to the whereabouts of his son's spirit. In his heartfelt book, *My Life after*

Life: A Posthumous Memoir, Dr. Stoller wrote honestly how this experience would change his credibility and reputation as a physician. However, for him, truth was the catalyst for writing the book, and this was a love story between a father and son. What differentiates Dr. Stoller from most physicians is that in the early 1970, he has the opportunity to volunteer at the UCLA Neuropsychiatric Institute. While there, he was able to observe the work of trance mediums, so he had a greater understanding of the ability to communicate with others outside their physical body.

For myself, that was one of the first things I said. "I want to know where my son is. If energy can never be destroyed, where did he go?" Dr. Stoller's story is one of hope, inspiration, and understanding. He discovered that he can communicate with his son; in fact, they wrote the book together! Dr. Stoller's story is one worth reading.

See **https://www.griefsos.com/founder**.

SUSANNE WILSON

Susanne had been in the corporate world for many years as an executive. Although she knew she was different and could sense spirit, it blossomed after she had an NDE in a doctor's office while being tested for allergies.

Her mediumship ability was tested at the University of Arizona under strict controls, and was hailed by Gary Schwartz, Ph.D. as one of the best. My first exposure to Susanne was at the 2015 AREI conference in Scottsdale. She spoke about her abilities with humor and quickly changed the energy of many audience members from sorrow to laughter. She offered a few readings to the crowd and demonstrated her innate ability to communicate with the other side.

A month later, I heard Susanne speak at a local bookstore in Phoenix. She included a few readings to audience members, saying that our loved ones were politely lining up to give her messages. Sean was the first in line. Her validations mitigated any doubt that she was talking directly with Sean.

I was fortunate to have several readings with Susanne throughout the years, and at one point, she allowed Sean to take over and speak directly to me through her. It was just like the many phone calls he and I shared in the past, and I will never forget it.

Susanne is known as the Carefree Medium because she resides in Carefree, Arizona. Her contact information can be found at **https://carefreemedium.com/**.

VICTOR ZAMMIT, LLB

A native of Australia, Victor Zammit worked as an attorney in the local, district, and supreme courts in Sydney. For many years, his main interests were human rights and social justice. After numerous clairvoyant and clairaudient experiences, Victor began to investigate the afterlife. Due to his legal training, his research resulted in evidence that is more than circumstantial. With his wife, Wendy, he published *A Lawyer Presents Evidence for the Afterlife* in 2013.

I was honored to meet Victor at the 2015 AREI conference in Scottsdale. He has offered anyone $1,000,000 if they can prove conclusively than there is no survival of consciousness after death. To date, no one has collected the money. The preface and conditions are explained here: **http://www.victorzammit.com/skeptics/challenge.html**.

WENDY ZAMMIT, M.A.

Wife of Victor, Wendy Zammit is an afterlife researcher and a professional counselor. With her husband, she co-authors the free weekly "Friday Afterlife Report," (**http://www.victorzammit.com/archives/index.html**). There is always new information and data to support their lifelong undertaking. I enjoy the way Wendy and Victor present as partners; each has a love and respect for the other and afterlife research. Together, they break down the information into digestible bites, so that anyone can understand and assimilate their research.

You can find more information about Wendy Zammit here: **http://mind-studies.com/wendy-zammit-m/**.

www.ingramcontent.com/pod-product-compliance
Lightning Source LLC
Chambersburg PA
CBHW042117100526
44587CB00025B/4090